CAMBRIDGE LIBRARY COLLECTION

Books of enduring scholarly value

History

The books reissued in this series include accounts of historical events and movements by eye-witnesses and contemporaries, as well as landmark studies that assembled significant source materials or developed new historiographical methods. The series includes work in social, political and military history on a wide range of periods and regions, giving modern scholars ready access to influential publications of the past.

Military Service and Adventures in the Far East

This two-volume work, published in 1847 by cavalry officer Daniel Henry Mackinnon (1813–84) describes his military service in India, in the campaigns against the Afghans in 1839 and the Sikhs in 1845–6. In the first edition, reissued here, the author is referred to only as 'a cavalry officer', but in the second edition of 1849, Mackinnon, a career soldier and writer, abandons his anonymity. Volume 1 begins with a lively account of the Andaman Islands, before 'arrival in India' at Calcutta and a long march past the foothills of the Himalayas to the North-West Frontier province. Mackinnon fought at the decisive battle of Ghuzni in the First Anglo-Afghan War, and provides an eye-witness account of the storming of the city, though his description of the political and diplomatic conflicts which preceded the outbreak of the wars is somewhat simplistic, and inevitably Anglophile.

Cambridge University Press has long been a pioneer in the reissuing of out-of-print titles from its own backlist, producing digital reprints of books that are still sought after by scholars and students but could not be reprinted economically using traditional technology. The Cambridge Library Collection extends this activity to a wider range of books which are still of importance to researchers and professionals, either for the source material they contain, or as landmarks in the history of their academic discipline.

Drawing from the world-renowned collections in the Cambridge University Library and other partner libraries, and guided by the advice of experts in each subject area, Cambridge University Press is using state-of-the-art scanning machines in its own Printing House to capture the content of each book selected for inclusion. The files are processed to give a consistently clear, crisp image, and the books finished to the high quality standard for which the Press is recognised around the world. The latest print-on-demand technology ensures that the books will remain available indefinitely, and that orders for single or multiple copies can quickly be supplied.

The Cambridge Library Collection brings back to life books of enduring scholarly value (including out-of-copyright works originally issued by other publishers) across a wide range of disciplines in the humanities and social sciences and in science and technology.

Military Service and Adventures in the Far East

*Including Sketches of the Campaigns
Against the Afghans in 1839,
and the Sikhs in 1845–6*

VOLUME 1

DANIEL HENRY MACKINNON

CAMBRIDGE
UNIVERSITY PRESS

CAMBRIDGE UNIVERSITY PRESS

Cambridge, New York, Melbourne, Madrid, Cape Town,
Singapore, São Paolo, Delhi, Mexico City

Published in the United States of America by Cambridge University Press, New York

www.cambridge.org
Information on this title: www.cambridge.org/9781108045780

© in this compilation Cambridge University Press 2012

This edition first published 1847
This digitally printed version 2012

ISBN 978-1-108-04578-0 Paperback

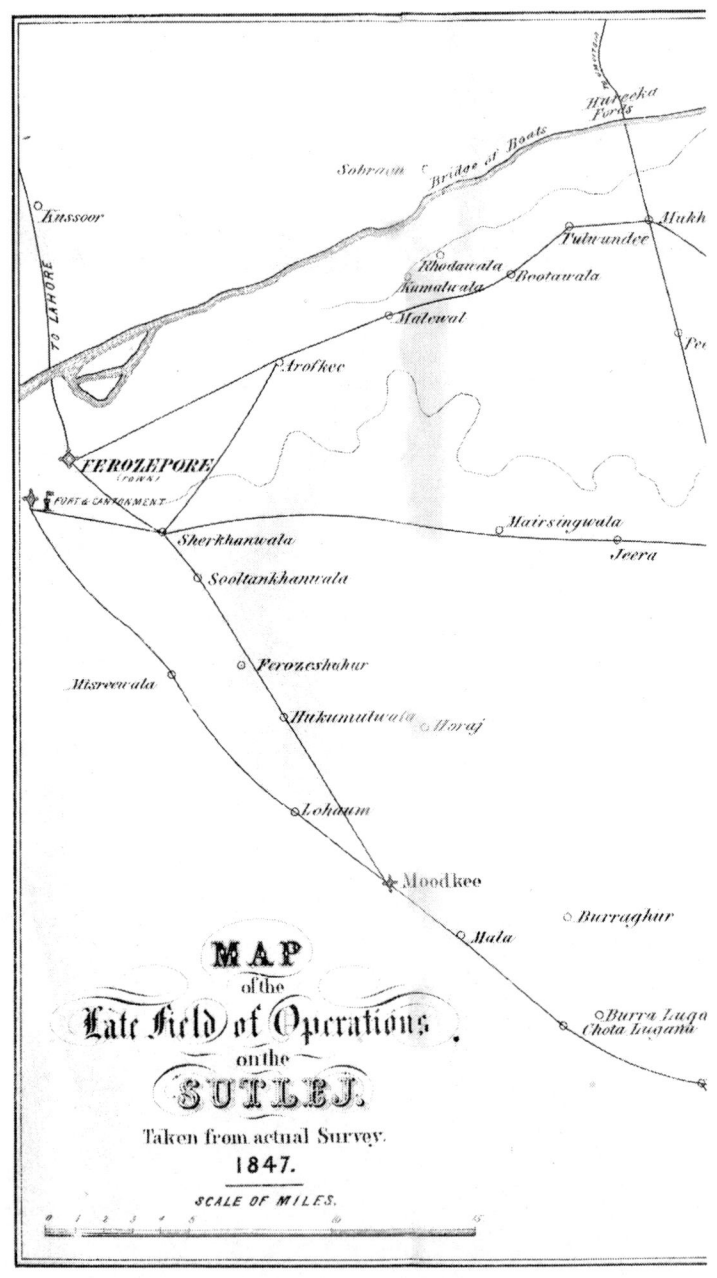

MAP

of the

Late Field of Operations.

on the

SUTLEJ.

Taken from actual Survey.

1847.

SCALE OF MILES.

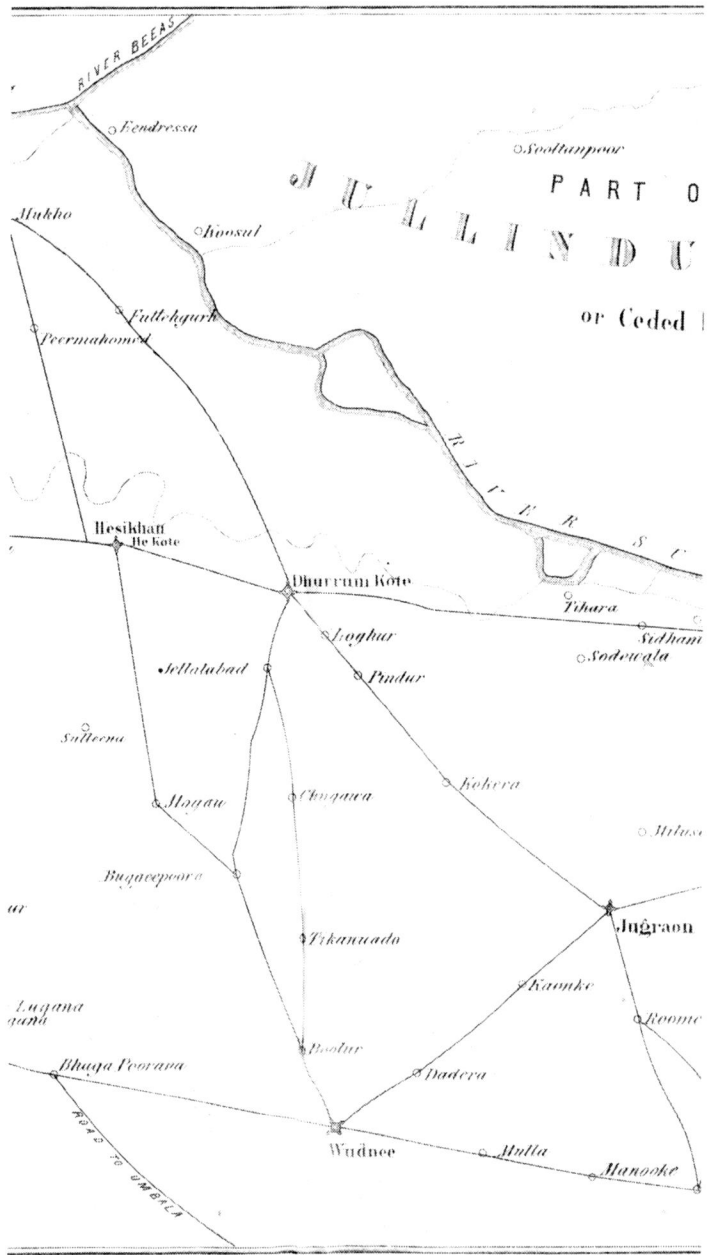

PART O

JULLINDU

or Ceded

RIVER BEEAS

Fendressa

Sooltanpoor

Mukho

Kiosul

Fattehgurh

Peermahomed

Hesikhan
He Kote

Dhurrum Kote

Vihara

Loghur

Sidham

Sodewala

Jellalabad

Pindur

Sulteena

Mogau

Chngawa

Kohera

Milas

Buqaeepoora

Jugraon

Tikanuado

Kaonke

Lugana
gana

Roome

Bhaga Poorava

Bootur

Dadera

Wudnee

Mulla

Manooke

ROAD TO UMBALA

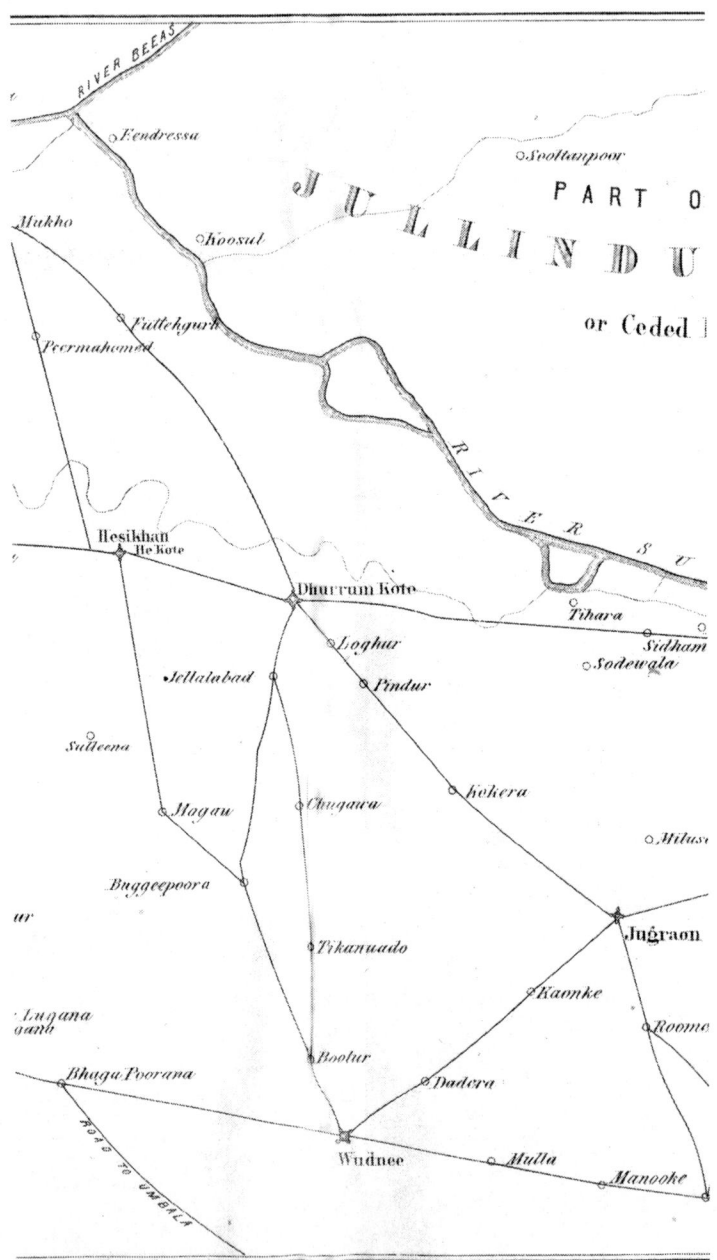

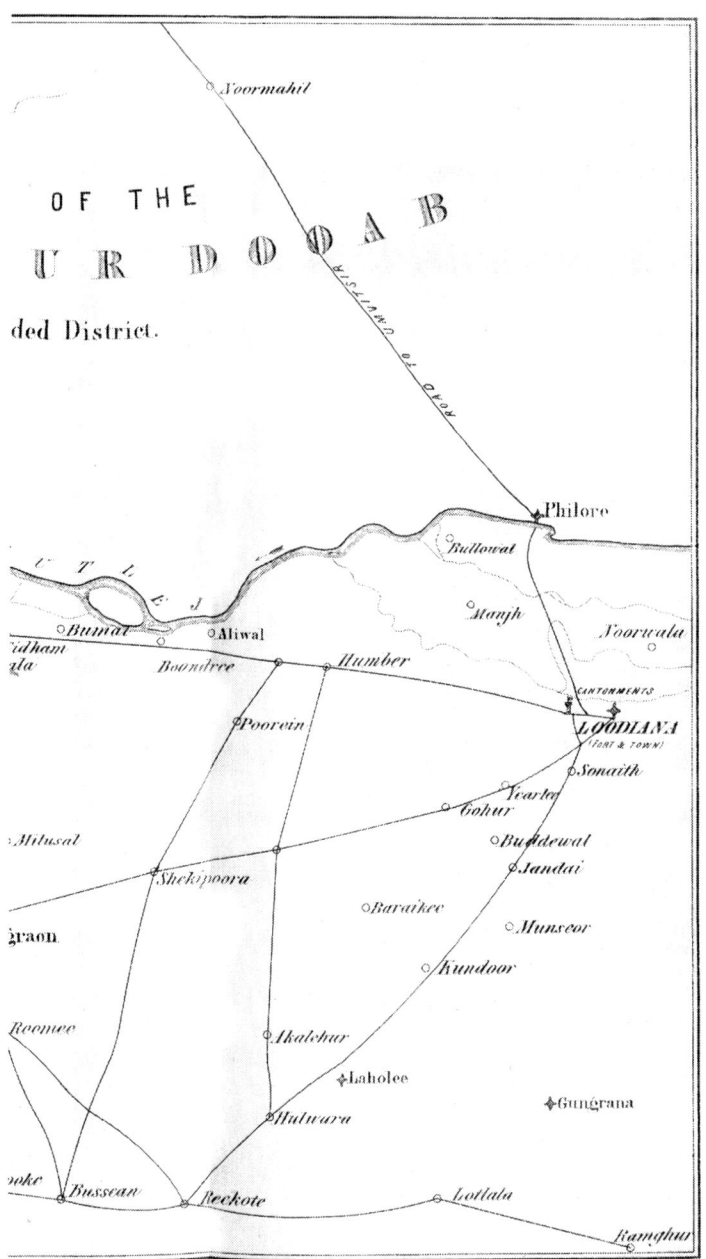

MILITARY SERVICE

AND

ADVENTURES IN THE FAR EAST:

INCLUDING

SKETCHES OF THE CAMPAIGNS

AGAINST THE AFGHANS IN 1839,

AND THE SIKHS IN 1845-6.

BY A CAVALRY OFFICER.

IN TWO VOLUMES.

VOL. I.

LONDON:

CHARLES OLLIER,

SOUTHAMPTON STREET, STRAND.

1847.

CONTENTS OF VOL. I.

MILITARY SERVICE

IN THE FAR EAST.

CHAPTER I.

ANY one who has coasted the Andamans will bear witness to the beauty of those Islands, of which, at the time I visited them, marvellous tales were related. The predilection of the inhabitants of those realms for their white brethren, when shipwrecked on these shores, was said to have been evinced in a manner singularly contrasted to other philanthropists, for they actually devoured them. It has moreover been stated, that the biped islanders were not the only philanthropists dwelling in these alluring scenes, but that the woods swarmed with a variety of wild beasts, who were also epicures in human flesh. It is, indeed, wonderful that man, being so great a luxury, should continue to exist in such regions. Unfortunately, we were unable to put any reports to the test, not having set foot ashore.

The sun, which had been shining brilliantly all the morning over these green isles, became obscured in the afternoon, when a breeze springing up soon caused a musical ripple of the waters, and wafted us in four days to the Sandheads; where, receiving our pilot on board, we coasted the low sandy ridge of Saugar, and anchored off Kedgeree, there to await the steamer which was to tow us up the Hoogly to the capital.

No sooner was our anchor dropped, than the river suddenly swarmed with boats full of the wildest-looking savages, in a perfect state of nature, saving a dingy clout bound about their waists. The hair hung like horses' tails over the shoulders of some; others had gathered up and twisted the sable mass into a knot on the top of their heads, which led us into considerable doubt as to the gender of the individuals, this being the generally approved method of arranging the hair amongst the ladies of our northern climes. But we did injustice, in this instance, to the more gentle and better sex, who in this region are as superior in shape and feature to the males, as an

English woman is to every other on the face of the earth! Nevertheless, these dusky anatomies possessed singularly Stentorian lungs, as we experienced when they came whooping and jabbering alongside.

Our worthy mate, being thoroughly versed in savage intercourse, loudly exclaimed, " Ho! you d—d Dinghee Wallahs! nickal jao there, will you? Quartermaster, hand up a bit of pork, heave it into that boat astern, and shove off those shoals at the gangway."

The sovereign remedy, a bit of pork, was carefully distributed among the boats, and relieved us of their presence; for when the savoury morsel alighted, they cast off, eyeing us with as much sorrowful disgust as the bit of unclean animal, which was taken up by one of the boatmen between two sticks, thrown overboard, and the polluted spot well scoured with the mud and water of the brown Hoogly.

In the afternoon, I went ashore, at Kedgeree, with a party of officers, to shoot. We wandered in various directions over the marshy rice fields, and through the low jungle, in quest of game: most of us loaded one barrel with small shot, and the other with ball, being uncertain as to the probability of meeting with a tiger or a snipe in

those unknown regions; but fortune having con-
ceded neither, we returned at nightfall to the appointed rendezvous for re-embarking, and found
the ship's boats had returned on board: our two
linguists had gone with them. As it was getting
pitch dark, our prospects of a comfortable night's
rest were becoming correspondingly gloomy. In
these straits, we wandered along the banks to a
village, where, endeavouring to make the natives
aware of our wants by signs, they immediately
brought us some fruits, making countersigns for
money; that and food being pretty nearly the sum
total of their worldly concernments. At this
juncture, one of our party returned from a successful forage, having found a tent occupied by a
European.

We hastened readily to the canvas abode, and
our deliverer having treated us to a few tumblers
of cold water, and explained our wishes to the
natives, in a few minutes we each mounted our
savage, and rode him over the mud and water to
a canoe moored near the bank.

An hour's hard rowing, enlivened, at times, by
the wild and discordant singing, or rather yelling,
of our swarthy boatmen, brought us once more
alongside the ship, anything but pleased with our
first excursion on the shores of Hindostan.

I am persuaded that the phosphorescent appearance which we often observe on the ocean, must hold some invisible and fiery influence over the minds of those whose business for a time is on the great waters. To this cause I venture to attribute the strong matrimonial epidemic which broke out on board our trusty ship, many marriages being meditated, and some celebrated by certain of my fellow-passengers. The gaiety which ought to be consequent on weddings was not, at first, very perceptible; but this, I take it, was mainly attributable to the nautical stomach-pump, which took severe effect during the first fortnight, principally, (I lament to say,) on the fair sex. The operations of this fearful tormentor at length ceased. Had the immortal Lawrence Sterne but enjoyed the advantages of a voyage to India, what a mighty field would have been thrown open for the indulgence of his favourite reflections to the edification of his readers and advancement of natural philosophy. But he and his class have long passed from among us, and I must leave to such as deem themselves competent to the task, the elucidation of a theory, (holding doubtless the most absolute influence over the intricate human system,) a subject far too abstruse for this feeble pen.

Having spent two days at anchor off Kedgeree, on the third morning we joyfully descried a dark little steamer, which, though more resembling a demon than a saint, proved our deliverer from the shoals of the muddy Hoogly.

The slimy banks of the river, fringed at a short distance from the water with stunted jungle, gradually gave place to a more civilized appearance as we advanced up the stream; and on rounding Garden Reach, the view was eminently beautiful. The neat villas of the Calcutta merchants, now partially hidden amongst their gardens and shrubberies, and now bursting full upon the view—the river, with the ceaseless stir of business skimming across its waters, and the distant prospect of the city of palaces, flanked by a forest of bare and taper masts, presented altogether a picture of exciting interest, especially to one about to set foot for the first time in a new country, and, to him, almost a new world.

We came to anchor, on the third morning after quitting Kedgeree, under the walls of Fort William, and found H. M.'s third Dragoons encamped on the glacis. About four in the afternoon, the heat having considerably abated, we disembarked, and marched into the Fort, where quarters had been provided for our men, though none for the officers, as the brigade-major informed us, at the same time stating, that as a difference of opinion existed on that subject between himself and the fort-major, we must wait until he (of the Queen's) had craftily overcome him (of the Company's), and induced the latter individual to house us.

There is an old proverb about a man between two stools being likely to come to the ground, which was fully illustrated in our case, for, both of our supports for a night's rest in Fort William having given way, we came to the earth, though fortunately in the tents of the 3rd Dragoons, immediately under the walls of the fort, where our fall was kindly broken by cloaks spread on the ground to receive us.

I was composing myself to sleep as comfortably as circumstances would permit, when suddenly a volley of screams, as though proceeding from the lungs of ten thousand demons, caused me to start on my feet, supposing the camp to have been invaded by the infernal regions. My host, lying in the opposite recess of the tent, being a man of some days' experience, begged me not to disturb myself, as it was only the jackals. " Only the jackals!" but they are pretty nearly enough to murder sleep, I thought, as I laid myself down to await the cessation of their intolerable howls.

Silence at length ensued, and I was just falling asleep, when a low gurgling noise arose close to my ears, and continued with the most monotonous regularity: "Good Heaven!" I cried, after listening intently for a few minutes, "that must come from the diabolical bandicoots, of which I have often heard from old Indians." I drew my sword, and awaited their advance in a violent perspiration, for I have an insuperable abhorrence to the whole rat tribe; but they had no intention of coming to close quarters. No, their cursed pipes sounded the advance, unheeded by the main body. My enemies, nevertheless, seemed to be mustering; for the gurgle was taken up by a reinforcement from the opposite side of the tent, interrupted occasionally by a low, muttering sound:

"Jam jam efficaci do manus scientiæ.

"I submit; it is impossible to sleep through this interminable persecution, and a man's days in this climate must be necessarily short without rest!" Thus I exclaimed, as, jumping up, I threw my cloak aside, and paced the tent in a fever, saluted incessantly by the unearthly gurgle.

My friend lay on the opposite side, sleeping as calmly as if there were no such things in the world to torture us as jackals or bandicoots.

The morning was just breaking, and I stepped out of the tent, in hope of being taken for a ghost by the jackals, and thus retaliating by fright on a portion of my enemies—when, lo! the veil of mystery was withdrawn, and there sat two Hindoos smoking the pipe of the country, commonly known by the name of hubble-bubble, which noisy instrument I had mistaken all night for the bandicoots.

This was too absurd. I burst into a fit of laughter, which awakened my friend, who hastily joined me, when I related my grievance. Having silenced the smokers, I soon enjoyed the rest I had almost despaired of attaining.

The following day, having stated our houseless condition to Sir Willoughby Cotton, commanding the division, we were, by his order, allotted quarters in the Fort, where the bugs and mosquitoes were as unwelcome visitants as the jackals and hubble-bubbles of the preceding night.

Having procured some native servants, deposited our baggage in the barracks, and bought large cane bedsteads with mosquito curtains, we began to consider ourselves in clover, though our ignorance of Hindustani left us completely at the mercy of the natives, my sirdar (valet) being not of the most intelligent order. At night, when he had succeeded in clearing my bed of mosquitoes, and carefully arranged the curtains, I signed to him to take away the light. He immediately left the room, but took not the candle. "Sirdar!" He immediately re-entered. I telegraphed him with much energy, pointing to the candle and thence to the door. He shook his head and looked bewildered. This was not to be endured; I darted out of bed to extinguish the light; and a colony of mosquitoes, who had been awaiting this opportunity, immediately established themselves inside, and conversed with me during the night.

Notwithstanding our numerous tormentors, the season of the year at which we landed was the coolest and most salubrious of any—that is, the mornings were coldest, and the mid-day heat was also at its minimum; but even a December sun, at noon, was not to be encountered with impunity.

I sallied forth in one of those coffin-like conveyances termed palanquins, to visit the city, which is about a mile distant from the fort, and extends along the banks of the river. Enormous store-houses and merchants' offices skirt the river;

but the interior of the city, and especially that portion adjacent to the plain around Fort William contains several fine public buildings and extensive private mansions. The streets and squares are wide and handsome; but the bazaars and the portion of the town tenanted by natives are wretchedly narrow and confined, and usually thronged nearly to suffocation; for the natives love to huddle together in contradistinction to the whites, who seem even on this broiling and dreary side of the world to preserve that cold and forbidding demeanour which distinguishes the English in particular from other nations of the globe.

I believe the case was materially different a few years ago; but we found cause to remark, during our fortnight's sojourn in Calcutta, that we had experienced less hospitality and more incivility than in any other city of the world, not excepting even New York. The then revolution in the social system of the East has been attributed to the recent establishment of hotels in the city, but this appears more of a subterfuge than a palliation. The absence of the governor-general and commander-in-chief, who were at that time in the upper provinces, had drained Calcutta of the best of its population, as we were informed and afterwards experienced; and we therefore saw the place under unfavourable circumstances.

After a comfortless delay of a fortnight, in this city of contrasted luxury and indigence, we gladly received the route to march for our destination in the north-western provinces.

Having provided ourselves with tents, and bullock hackeries for the conveyance of them and our baggage, we left Calcutta about sunrise on the 4th January, and marched along the banks of the river, through avenues of cocoa-nut and palm trees, to our first encampment, a distance of about ten miles.

Our party mustered nearly five hundred strong, and included detachments for all of her Majesty's regiments in the upper provinces. Both officers and privates were, almost to a man, commencing their first march in India, or, to use an Indian expression, "griffins;" and in consequence many forebodings had been uttered, in Calcutta, of depredations, blunders, and miseries we were to encounter: "mais il est plus facile d'être sage pour les autres, que de l'être pour soi-même," saith Rochefoucauld, and with truth, in the present instance, for we encountered few of the ills presaged by the Indian prophets, who had probably drawn their conclusions from sad experience.

The second morning we marched in the dark, and reached the river Hoogly about daylight. The transit occupied the greater portion of the day, having to unload the beasts of burden and convey the men and baggage in boats. The most interesting and novel sight to us was that of the huge elephants swimming across this broad and rapid river, with the mahout, or driver, standing or sitting on their necks. Immediately the elephant gets beyond his depth, his whole body and head disappear, and nothing is seen to mark his locale, save the head and shoulders of the mahout. The obedient monster performs the submarine passage with an occasional jerk of the head and trunk out of water, to take breath and see where he is going, although in the latter instance he is generally subservient to his driver.

Some accidents were nearly occurring from the elephants having been swept down by the current among the boats in which the troops were crossing, but the mahouts piloted their charges dexterously through the fleet, without a single collision.

After crossing the Hoogly, we marched, for the first few days, through a well cultivated country, but afterwards struck into a newly made road, lying amid thick low jungle, until we reached the Rajmahal hills, which in some places are thickly and prettily wooded, whilst the intervening plains and valleys diversify the scene with their irregular patches of Indian corn, sugar cane, and barley fields. The Rajmahal hills abound with bears, tigers, wild hog, and elephants; but all chance of sport in wild beast hunting was denied us; we had no shikar wallahs, or sporting elephants among our party; for in India it is quite as necessary—nay, more so—that the elephant should be a sporting character as the rider, for the uninitiated usually dread the sight of a wild beast, and at the critical moment of encounter the unhappy sportsman often finds himself involuntarily taking to an ignominious flight. It is impossible to beat the heavy coverts of this part of India, with a moderate chance of success, except on elephants. Our principal amusement during the whole march consisted in partridge and snipe shooting, and even these were exceedingly scarce in the neighbourhood of our camp; but this was on account of the distance we generally kept from the Ganges, the banks of which are well supplied with game. In fact, throughout India, game is rarely found anywhere save in the vicinity of rivers, theels, or inundated ground.

Our friends, the jackals, continued their nightly lamentations, varied occasionally by the deep bass of a bear, or hyæna's eccentric cry ; but I heard of only one actual encounter between man and beast in the Rajmahals, which was between an infantry soldier and a bear, beside the stump of an old tree, which both approached, unconscious of each other's presence, to use as a seat. Having eyed one another with feelings of mutual aversion, they executed a chassée-croisée, and parted. When a bear is desirous of being on intimate terms with a man, he rears himself on his hind legs, and advances to embrace, but the cruel sportsman marks, with his keen eye, a white mark on the affectionate creature's breast, and repays the advance by a bullet sent through this vital spot—that is, if his hand be steady enough to execute the act of ingratitude.

On emerging from the hills, we marched over an almost uninterrupted plain, which preserves the same smooth features almost to the very foot of the Himalayahs.

After an uninteresting and monotonous march of four hundred miles, which occupied about six weeks, always halting on Sundays, the first military station we reached was the sacred city of Benares. Here we crossed the Ganges, above whose muddy waters we descried the minarets of the holy places towering in the cloudless sky, and, from their lofty relief, rendering more apparent the insignificance of the low mud and brick dwelling-places clustered around their bases.

The cantonments lie about four miles from the city, laid out with strict military precision : most of the officers' bungalows thatched with dry grass, standing in the midst of their square compounds, enclosed by a high mud wall.

Even the native soldiers are different looking beings from their unenlisted brethren, and stalk along with the conscious importance of improved condition.

The roads, which are made of concha,* are broad and excellent, and everything wears an air of starch discipline.

Near the cantonment lived a Madras rajah, who, having been deprived of his power and estates in that presidency, had been transplanted here and pensioned by government. With the customary adulation of the East, he readily licks the hands of his oppressors, apes English manners, and courts English society.

I accompanied a brother officer, who had been previously acquainted with him, to the rajah's

* Concha is a species of siliceous clay, lying in strata at a depth of from three to four feet beneath the surface of the whole alluvial plain of the Ganges.

mansion, which was a comfortable residence, without any attempt at magnificence. The room into which we were ushered was adorned with pictures representing the victories of Wellington, Nelson, and Napoleon. After keeping us some time waiting, his highness at length made his appearance. He was a tall, sallow-complexioned man, attired in a white frock coat, black silk handkerchief, brown silk pajamas,* and red morocco slippers. Supposing the principal means of entertaining Englishmen to be the satisfying of their appetites, he lost not a minute in introducing us to the supper-table, where he begged us to be seated, setting the example himself—at least, if his might be termed an example, for he perched himself most uncomfortably on the extreme edge of a large arm-chair, and with the assistance of its arms and his own, managed to preserve a very precarious equilibrium.

As it is very difficult for a person to feel at ease when he perceives that his companion is not, I hoped every instant to see him glide from the chair, and squat on the floor, in the position natural to his countrymen, but he did not, in this instance, gratify us or himself.

* Pajamas are loose trousers.

Supper being over, we adjourned to an inner room, where, to my surprise, we were presented to his wife and daughters. The former was about thirty years of age, glittering with jewels, and retaining visible proofs of having been a beauty in her day. Her eldest daughter, about thirteen years of age, (advanced womanhood in India,) was the most perfect dark beauty I have ever seen: her figure was slight, yet round and elegant—as are those of most Indian women of high caste; an invidious veil covered the greater portion of her glossy hair, but her clear olive complexion, and lustrous black eyes—too dazzling to be looked on with impunity — were a *chef-d'œuvre* of Nature. Never, till that night, did I bitterly repent my neglect of the Hindustani tongue.

The rajah told us that he fully intended to pass the evening of his days in England, where his beautiful daughter, with her ample dowry, will probably become the victim of some expert adventurer.

Having halted two days at Benares, we proceeded through as uninteresting a country as before, passing, occasionally, a mud town or village, with the usual appendages of a small grove of trees and a few square patches of cultivation round the wells, whilst two or three hundred natives, huddled together, and squatted like so many vultures on the walls and by the roadside, watched our onward progress, and chattered their rapid jargon.

Ten marches from Benares we again crossed the Ganges where it unites its polluting waters with those of the rocky and clear Jumna, and entered the cantonments of Allahabad. The fort commands a view of the two rivers as they flow onwards to their junction, immediately under its walls; but excepting these waters, the eye wanders over a continued parched and arid plain, save where a small grove of trees presents occasionally a relieving object.

The festival of the Mohurrem was about to take place as we quitted Allahabad. The scenes of riot and debauchery annually consequent on this as well as other festivals, have entailed a lasting disgrace on the government of India, which not only tolerates, but actually encourages them. Nor has it scrupled to convert the superstition of the deluded natives into a substantial accession to the revenues of the country. Those who may be affected with any scruples on this subject, possibly reconcile the matter to their conscience by the disbursement of a few rupees

annually for the maintenance of a handful of
missionaries to convert the people of India to
Christianity ; but it will require something more
than the present feeble efforts to accomplish that
object, and possibly a little more sincerity in the
authors of such an endeavour. In these modern
days of toleration, it will hardly answer to follow
the policy of the Emperor Julian towards the
early Christians, and apply it to the Mussulman
or Hindoo—as, when the emperor says, " I show
myself the true friend of the Galileans. Their
admirable law has promised the kingdom of
heaven to the poor, and they will advance with
more diligence and virtue in the paths of salva-
tion when they are relieved, by my assistance,
from the load of temporal possessions." *

The dust on the road between Allahabad and
Cawnpore passeth all understanding. The head
of our column got along tolerably well, not sinking much above their knees in the impalpable
soil ; but the centre and rear staggered blindly
onward, and not unfrequently downward, through
the clouds raised by their predecessors, till they
reached more substantial ground ; others jostled
against mud walls and trees, trod on their neigh-

---

* Julian, Ep. xliii. Gibbon, ii. 48.

bour's toes, or, wandering from their comrades, groped their way out of the dense atmosphere, and only discovered the locality of the column by the glimpse of a few miller-like objects preceding the cloud.

Ten marches from Allahabad, over roads of the above description, and through a country which, being hid by a dusty screen, I seldom saw, and cannot therefore describe, brought us into the cantonments of Cawnpore, which appear to rise like a city in the desert. Not a tree was to be seen, and scarce a vestige of animal or vegetable life was presented to our view, as the morning broke upon us crossing the arid and almost trackless plain near Cawnpore. At length, when the sun arose, a dim line of conical objects was descried through the lurid atmosphere, and, at the same time, the roar of some half-dozen pieces of cannon, at practice on the plain, announced the vicinity of cantonments.

Here the men of the detachments were placed in barracks, and the officers' tents pitched in a compound, where the sun blazed fiercely enough to roast a live lobster in his shell, though, from our species of that animal, nothing was elicited beyond moisture and murmuring.

Three days having been passed in this eligible

situation, I was despatched up the country with my own detachment and sundry others for regiments in the north-western provinces, an escort of a havildar* and twelve Sepoys having been provided to *take charge* of us, which trust they faithfully performed.

At this time, a dreadful famine was prevalent in the districts through which we passed, which was fearfully evidenced by the appalling sights we daily witnessed on the march. Living skeletons crowded round us in thousands, stretching forth their meagre hands and supplicating relief with countenances which beggared description. Scarcely a mile of ground was passed without seeing some wretched creature breathing his last by the road-side, or some, whose sufferings ended, were affording a scanty meal to the famished Pariah dogs. All caste and heathenish scruples were overcome by the craving for food, and the poor creatures tore each other in the avidity with which they scrambled for bones or offal thrown to them by the soldiers. The myriads which thronged our camp became a crying nuisance; and the dictates of humanity were so far repressed by the calls of duty and necessity, that I was

* A havildar is the serjeant of a native regiment.

compelled to encircle our small encampment with
a chain of sentries to exclude them, and prevent
their diseases from spreading amongst our own
camp.

No permanent relief could be afforded by our
people, and the bestowal of a morsel here and
there was merely a protraction of suffering.
About fifty miles from Cawnpore, and on the
banks of the former bed of the Ganges, are the
ruins of Kanoge, formerly one of the principal
cities of India, and by some supposed to have
been the limit of Alexander the Great, in his
Eastern campaign.*

Above the congregated heaps of mud and brick
are seen the white domes of monuments and
temples of later construction, like the ghosts of
decayed Eastern grandeur peering out on the
surrounding desolation. The vicinity of an ancient ruin incites most of us to a contemplative
mood. We reflect on the scenes that have been
enacted there when the building was tenanted,
and its inmates were playing their part on the
stage of life. It is true, that the events of those

* Kanoge was built about 1000 years B.C., and *was said*
to exceed 100 miles in circumference; it was besieged by
Mahmoud of Ghuzni, and surrendered about A.D. 1020.—
(R. Dow's Works.)

days we have wandered back upon, may not have been a whit more interesting than those at present before us; yet Time generally hallows the past with a certain veneration, especially when connected with associations of classical antiquity such as may be conjured up in Kanoge; and the faintest evidence may lead us to walk on the track of the mighty Macedonian, and think—

> " Hic illius arma—
> Hic currus fuit."

The atmosphere of Kanoge certainly conveys a sense of desolation surpassing that of any other ruinous city I have visited, and mutely explains its fallen condition unaided by native legends or speculative historians. I have read many discussions on the present and past state of this city; but none, I am convinced, could have visited it at a more impressive period than I did, when a dreadful famine was testifying itself in the faces and forms of the scanty, emaciated inhabitants.

Advancing up the country, we found during nearly every march a grove of trees sufficiently extensive to encamp under, which sheltered us considerably from the sun and dust, both of which were becoming seriously disagreeable, especially the latter, which rose daily about noon, with the wind setting in at that time, and lasted till sunset, when it dropped, leaving everything in the tent buried an inch deep in dust; and then came our ancient enemies the mosquitoes.

Three weeks marching carried us over two hundred miles of country, and to a town called Koorja, within sixty miles of Merut, where we experienced a severe typhoon, which, though of common occurrence in Upper India, was the first I had seen, and the most destructive that had been felt that season. It came on suddenly about four in the afternoon, having given us no notice of its approach, for the appearance all round had been hazy during the afternoon. In five seconds, we were enveloped in complete darkness, caused by clouds of sand and dust raised by the tempest, and whirled through the air. The howling of the storm was accompanied by almost incessant peals of thunder. As the typhoon increased in violence, the fiery appearance of the dust, from the continued gleaming of lightning, presented a singular effect. In the course of a quarter of an hour, two tents were levelled and torn to pieces, and my own quivered to such a degree, that, expecting to be carried away with it, I got clear of the impending wreck, and, groping my way out to leeward, came immediately in contact with a huge bullock. Any port in a storm, thought I, as I clung to the monster's horns for an anchorage. He, like an unfeeling brute, struggled hard to get rid of the burden; and the contest was at the fiercest, when, coming in contact with a hackery, to which he was attached, we both rolled on the ground together. " Taree machee!" screamed an unhappy gharuwan,* against whom we fell; but his invective was cut short by a kick in the stomach from my antagonist. Rejoiced to find a more passive assistant in the hackery-wheels, I let go the refractory bullock, and held on by the cart until the storm abated. This took place in a few minutes; when, creeping from my shelter, amid a deluge of rain, into a portion of the tent that fortunately remained standing, I lay in comparative comfort, listening to the retiring rattle of the thunder.

We then set about repairing the damages of the camp, and soon put it in condition to afford shelter for the night.·

At daybreak, the whole country appeared one sheet of water, through which we marched; and, having lost our guide, soon afterwards lost our way. Having wandered some miles in search of

* Gharuwan—a bullock-driver.

a road, we came at length to a village, where, seizing upon an unwilling guide, we were by him conducted across country, or rather across water, to our destination.

The land assumed a more green and cheerful aspect for the last five marches into Merut, which we reached, without any further accidents, on the 10th of April.

As the hot winds, which are not agreeable " compagnons de voyage," were daily expected to set in, we congratulated ourselves on the conclusion of this long and weary march of nearly nine hundred miles, which was accomplished in ninety-six days.

Although the labours of the march were ended, I felt myself far from comfortable in my new quarters, for the greater part of my baggage was on the Ganges—some eight hundred miles off; I was not settled in any habitation ; and lastly, I was among strangers : the two latter objections were soon overcome, but the former I found a serious inconvenience.

No life of which I can form an estimate, even that on board ship, can present fewer attractions than a residence, during the hot season, in India. In the upper provinces, about the end of April, the hot winds come rushing from the sandy deserts to the westward, bearing on their fiery wings columns of burning dust, which penetrate to every room in the house, and replenish the eyes, ears, and mouth of the sufferer who ventures to face them faster than he can dispose of the nuisance. A framework of bamboos, covered with long roots of grass termed cuscus, is placed against the windows and doors to the westward, which are continually watered outside by a native, at the expense of keeping up his attention by an occasional "halloo." About sunset, the wind usually drops, and the air remains impregnated with particles of fiery red dust; and as that is the time for coming out of the heated dwelling to swallow the hotter air outside, we may as well change the subject, for it is not likely to prove interesting or agreeable.

Towards the end of June, these messengers of the desert cease to arrive ; a calm interval (but rather a *restless* calm) succeeds, which is shortly broken, if the season be favourable, by the approach of heavy columns of clouds from the east, which burst over the thirsty plains of India like angels' visits. The sensation of renovated existence conveyed by this first fall of rain both to animal and vegetable may be imagined even by those who have witnessed the rare effect of a short summer's drought in rainy England.

From the descriptions I had heard of our present quarters, I imagined Merut to be a most picturesque little elysium; but those accounts were generally spitefully uttered by discontented Indians, during a summer's drizzle or a London fog. The stern reality varied little from the character of other cantonments which I had visited during my march up the country, either in point of climate or scenery. The barracks are oblong, single-storied buildings, dressed with mathematical precision, (and conveying from a distance the idea of so many petrified columns of troops,) flanked with equally precise roads.

In rear of the men's barracks are arranged, in similar order, the officers' bungalows, each enclosed in a small square compound, the condition of which depends of course on the pursuits or taste of the owner.

The massive bungalow to the right of the line, is flanked by high mud walls, to which are appended dog-kennels on one side and extensive stables on the other. More care and attention have evidently been bestowed on this than on the dwelling-house. The available land, embellished by a patch of oats and a parterre of half-demolished lucerne, proclaims the owner an amateur of the turf and field.

The small, but neater-looking building at the further extremity of the line, situated in the midst of a garden, fragrant with many a variety of flower and carefully-pruned shrub, tell, beyond a doubt, that some benign influence has dispensed these blessings on the soil, whilst the house contains the gem itself:

> " In the cup of life,
> That honey drop—the virtuous wife."

Gardens overgrown with weeds, dilapidated walls and gates, testify the indolence or indifference of other owners ; and yonder drowsy-looking building, with most of its shutters closed, and the verandah piled with six dozen chests, beside which are reclining, in good-humoured repose, a numerous and motley group of *marines*, who have travelled from the generous vineyards of France and Germany to perform their last duty on the burning soil of Hindostan,—all these afford too strong evidence to require explanation.

The heat of the weather during June, this year, certainly exceeded anything I had ever anticipated, and its continuance day and night became deeply oppressive to the spirits of the uninitiated.

About the middle of the month, we had a smart shock of an earthquake, which was felt from Calcutta to the Himalayah mountains, although it caused little injury. The sensation was of a most singular and disagreeable nature, the roof of the house assuming a menacing attitude, and appearing to rock to and fro; but giddiness prevented me from being over particular in taking observations. A small cistern of water becoming violently agitated and overflowing its sides, was illustrative of what happened after the shock was over.

We were, at length, relieved from the violent and sickening heat, by a strong easterly breeze, bringing a mass of threatening clouds, which burst like a water-spout over the plains. In twenty-four hours, the cantonments and surrounding country were flooded, and the before arid plains now presented the appearance of an extensive lake. When the rains cease, and the clouds, rolling away, give place to the sun to look upon the waters, his influence soon dries a large portion of the soil, and the vapours which rise from the earth produce a damp heat, less endurable than the preceding dryness, and much more insalubrious.

After this change in the weather, I paid a visit

to the Himalayah mountains, which lie about a hundred and ten miles north of Merut, and presented a most tantalizing sight during the hot season, rearing their snow-capped peaks at apparently so short a distance from the scorched and glistening plains of our present quarters.

CHAPTER II.

VISIT TO THE HIMALAYAH MOUNTAINS.

OUR party, consisting of three officers of my regiment and myself, started on the evening of the 1st of August, and having halted during the heat of the next day at a house on the road, erected for the convenience of travellers by government, we reached the foot of the hills at daybreak on the 3rd instant.

We remained at a small inn recently established there, awaiting an interval in the torrents of rain which were descending, before we commenced our ascent. After the greater part of the day had passed without the occurrence of this lucid interval, I started with one of our party to mount the precipitous hills which towered above us, enveloped in mist. We procured two sturdy little mountain-

c 3

ponies, that despised our weight, and, dashing through the torrents of rain, breasted the rough acclivity. The mountains from Rajpore rise abruptly in a constant succession of sharp and lofty peaks, whose sides from beneath appear nearly perpendicular. The roads, which are about two yards in breadth, are cut round the sides of the mountains, and winding by a gradual ascent round some, conduct you slowly upwards; on others, the circuit being impeded, or too extensive for the former system, a zig-zag road is made, to bring you more rapidly, though much more laboriously, to their brow, whence a ridge frequently stretches across to the adjacent mountains.

The spirited little hill-ponies carried us fearlessly across these narrow passes, on each side of which a yawning abyss frequently descends, till lost to sight amid the gloomy shade of the rocks and shrubs projecting from its sides; whilst the mountain torrents, roaring above and beneath, and frequently dashing, in their impetuous course, across the path you are pursuing, present a wild and magnificent sight.

Night had far advanced, and our ponies began to exhibit unequivocal symptoms of weariness from their severe toil, when we arrived at the hotel, then standing at Mussouri, for the reception of travellers. Here we soon divested ourselves of our well-soaked garments, and enjoyed the unusual Eastern luxury of a blazing fire.

Next morning, the weather having cleared up, I sallied forth to enjoy the varied and beautiful scenery, and scrambled to the summit of Landour, which stands about 7000 feet above the level of the sea. On the front, towered the Tyne range, about 10,000 feet in height; and far beyond these, Jumnootri and Gungootri, whence flow the sources of the Jumna and Ganges, are visible, their summits glittering with everlasting snow, from an elevation of 24,000 feet. On the right of this barrier of eternal snow, was dimly visible the peak of Dwalagiri, whose hoary heights, though untrodden by the foot of mortal man, have been measured by his ingenuity, and pronounced to be the loftiest in the world.*

Dazzled with the resplendent and gorgeous scene, whose reflection from the morning sun became too much for the eye to endure, I turned to look down on the beautiful and fertile valley of the Doune, which lay stretched beneath, and through which the Ganges, extricating itself from the mountains, rushed, in its turbid and meander-

* The peak of Dwaligiri exceeds 27,000 feet.

ing course, into the plains; whilst on the other side of the same fairy valley, the clear and stately Jumma flowed majestically onwards, to unite its crystal waters with its sister river at Allahabad.

The scenery here is excessively striking to the traveller, on account of the miserably barren and uninteresting flats he must traverse ere reaching these mountains, which nature appears to have raised to a stupendous elevation, in atonement for her negligence to other parts of Hindostan. The mild climate of these regions has rendered them a favourite resort, during the summer months, for the families of those eking out their eastern servitude; and many neat villas, partaking more of the character of European than of Asiatic architecture, ornament the sides and summits of Landour and Mussouri. The woods, which cover with great luxuriance the lower ranges of hills, from the base to the summit, constitute the principal beauty of the mountains. The trees most abundant near Landour are the oak and rhododendron; the latter grows to a large size, and produces a rich crimson flower, far exceeding in size and brilliancy of colour the shrub producing that blossom in England; and in the spring so great is its abundance, that it appears to cast a ruddy hue on the sides of the mountains. In the interior of the mountains, I have seen, growing wild, almost every kind of fruit tree* met with in Europe. Here is also a very beautiful and gigantic fir growing in the higher altitudes, termed the deodar, which is peculiar, I believe, to the Himalayahs, and much valued for its durable properties when used in building.

The rains continued to fall with untiring assiduity until the latter part of September.

Early in October, I set out with a party of friends on a tour in the interior. We were each provided with a small tent holding a bed and table, which, in addition to our guns and a few bottles of wine and spirits, were all we could take with us; for so rugged and precipitous are the paths, that everything belonging to travellers in these mountains must be carried by the Paharries, (natives of the mountains,) who scramble up the steepest precipices with considerable loads strapped on their backs. There is generally much difficulty in procuring a quantum sufficit of these useful animals. The natives of the plains have a great aversion to the climate of the mountains, which usually disagrees with them, and

---

* I hear that botanists deny the unity of the genus.

cannot be made of much use in a journey in the interior. The Paharries, indeed, have a similar feeling towards the plains, and can seldom be prevailed on to remain any length of time in the lower regions.

From Landour we descended amongst the thick brushwood, and long tangled grass which clad the mountain sides until we reached the bottom of a kudd, or valley, not far above the level of the plains, through which foamed an impetuous mountain torrent. We had some difficulty in fording this stream, on account of its rapidity and the quantity of large moveable stones in its bed. Being surrounded by precipitous mountains, which completely intercepted every current of air, the heat in this valley was exceedingly oppressive. The vegetation around us was most luxuriant, and it was with considerable toil we forced our way through the wilderness of shrubs, interwoven with long matted grass.

We now commenced the abrupt ascent of the Tyne mountains, along a narrow Paharrie track, where the footing was extremely precarious, and a false step would have consigned the perpetrator to the tender mercies of the sharp pointed rocks several hundred feet beneath. About nightfall it became very difficult to distinguish the track, but our ponies, who scrambled along without any accidents behind us, seeming to make light of the matter, we mounted and trusted to their sagacity.

I had cause, ere long, to repent this misplaced confidence, for, on turning a sharp angle of rock, I was interrupted during an energetic argument with my successor by a most appalling stumble, and, in an instant, disappeared with my faithless quadruped, from the eyes of my astonished brother disputant.

A few feet under the ledge of rock grew a kind hearted shrub, (better deserving of immortality than the tree of murderous intentions upon Horace,) which I embraced and clung to with affectionate eagerness. My poor pony fared otherwise, and by the crashing amongst the stones and shrubs underneath, I had cause to conjecture he was suffering bitter punishment for his error : far from it, the fall had soon been converted into a roll, on the fortunately gradual slope of this especial spot, and we found him busily engaged with the thick grass which had preserved, and was now nourishing, the little viper.

The moon now made her appearance, and we reached a platform of land where fields of wheat and barley announced the vicinity of a village, whose mud huts we descried on the side of a steep ravine; above which towered a noble grove of the picturesque and lofty deodar. Under these we pitched our tents, and soon became unconscious alike of time and place.

Rising at daybreak, we recommenced the toilsome ascent, and, shortly after noon, reached the summit, whence was beheld an apparently endless range of mountain upon mountain, the nearest bristling with forests, the furthest hoary with snow. The description would be but a continual recurrence to the same imagery, so much does nature resemble herself in the drapery which she has spread on these wild regions.

Next morning, we commenced our preparations for the chase, and having each taken up a position, our dogs and Paharries entered the heavy cover, each giving tongue as the game started. The ear was now awake with intense expectation; the before-predominating silence was broken by echoed sounds.

The whirr of the gaudy pheasant as he sprang upwards from the covert, was succeeded by the roar of the murderous fowling-piece ringing his death-knell among his native hills; and the sharp crack of the rifle followed the track of the deer, as he dashed from the woods, and bounded wildly down the rocky precipices.

I had remained perched on my rock, contemplating the scene for a considerable time without being called upon to use my weapons, when suddenly a noble tehr* stood before me, his long dun hair hanging in ringlets over his body, and his head erect, listening to the cries of the beaters, now growing faint in the distance. I hastily snatched up my rifle, (as I thought,) and taking a steady aim at his shoulder, fired. Though barely forty yards from me, to my utter surprise, he dashed away unharmed, and in two minutes I saw him bounding at full speed along the ridge of a hill nearly a mile off. Turning away in silent disgust, I felt almost inclined to vent my anger on the rifle, but discovered that, in the haste of the moment, in lieu of the rifle I had snatched up a fowling-piece loaded with shot. Having lost an opportunity such as is rarely met with in tehr shooting, for they rank among the wildest of mountain game, I descended the hill in search of my companions, but they were far away, and I contented myself with the pursuit of small game.

At nightfall, our party straggled into camp, having all had but poor sport, which was a trifling consolation to me.

* The tehr is a mountain goat.

The game in these mountains, though of great variety, are exceedingly difficult to come at, owing to the heavy coverts which shelter them, and it is by no means singular for the best sportsmen to return empty handed. During my residence in the Himalayahs, I have frequently wandered the greater part of the day without meeting with a head of game—at other times, by being on the spot by day-break, I have succeeded in bringing down two or three chamois before sunrise. It is requisite to approach them with great caution, and always from above ; if the first ball be unsuccessful, the deer will sometimes wheel suddenly round, and stop from full speed to ascertain the reason of the interruption.

The gooral (or, more intelligibly speaking, the chamois) affords the best sport of all the mountain tribe. He is to be found early in the morning, feeding among the long grass, generally on the side of the steepest mountains, and must be carefully stalked, for his senses are of a refined order. When wounded, he often leads his destroyer a chase of many a weary mile down the steepest kudds, and over sharp pointed rocks, where the trail must be followed by the signs of the mountain dew brushed from the surface of the grass, or the rocks stained by the ebbing blood of the stricken animal. The sagacity of the Paharries in following this trail, and the sharpness of their sight, are very remarkable, in contradistinction to their neighbours of the plains ; but the fact is easily accounted for, from their having exercised these faculties in the chase from childhood amongst the same scenes, as they very seldom quit their native mountains. I have often seen a Paharrie detect, at the first glance, over a mountain, a gooral feeding on the further side, at a distance which took some landmark given me by my companion to ascertain the spot, and I have hardly ever known them to err. They are a hardy, active and courageous race, who, having been a most formidable foe to the British in the earlier periods of Indian warfare, have, now that they have enlisted under the banners of the Company, proved the bravest and best of the native army.

Many kinds of deer are to be found amongst the mountains, and an endless variety of the feathered tribe, amongst which the most remarkable are the distinct species of pheasants which haunt the mountains, the species varying with the altitude; but this subject is rather too plentiful a theme for the present narrative, and must be left to competent ornithologists.

The Jerrow, or maha, is the noblest specimen of the stag to be met with, and may be ranked as the elk of the Himalayah. He stands from four to five feet in height; his colour is a rich brown, and his antlers, branching into six on each side, have obtained for him the name of bara singh* in the plains. During the day time, they usually lie in the heaviest jungle; but at morning and evening they may be seen grazing in the rich pastures, and usually in pairs. The Jerrow, as he stalks majestically through the woods, bearing proudly aloft his high branching antlers, looks the undisputed monarch of the mountain forests.

The next in size to the Jerrow is a deer about three and a half feet in height at full growth, and termed the Surrow. He is of a dark hue, with short deflected horns, thickly built, and with coarse bristling hair, much like the wild hog. His head and shoulders resemble a donkey ornamentèd with a horse's mane and a goat's horns. This scarce and singular beast has a spirit in proportion to his deformity.

His habitation is among the gloomiest rocks and caverns, and when roused from his solitude he prepares readily for the conflict, and charges with desperate ferocity.

* Bara singh—twelve horns.

I remember an encounter between a brother-officer and sportsman, in the hills, and a surrow, which he had wounded, which nearly proved serious to the gallant and athletic soldier. M... threw himself upon the wounded animal, when he charged, and seized him in his iron grasp, so as to pinion the surrow and prevent his making use of his deadly antlers. The struggle continued a long time; the deer ultimately succeeded in getting his head free, and immediately struck savagely backwards with his horns, when M... narrowly escaped the fatal stroke, and casting himself sideways, grasped the surrow's neck with one arm, so that he could not use his horns with effect, while with the other he succeeded in drawing a clasp-knife, which put an end to the contest.

Besides the animals above mentioned, the Himalayahs can show to the persevering sportsman the small kaukur, or barking deer, the musk-deer, the hog deer, and in the snowy regions, the ibex, and burral, or wild sheep. The tiger and leopard frequent the deepest valleys of the lower ranges, and, late in the autumn, the bear-shooting of these mountains will rank with any sport that is to be met with in India.

I was preparing for the journey towards the sources of the Ganges, when a most unwelcome visitor, in the shape of a fever, summoned me homewards. It was in vain to struggle any longer with my obstinate antagonist, so I yielded to the advice of my fellow-travellers, and turned my back for ever on these wild and glorious mountains. The floor-cloth of my tent was taken up, and the two corners bound together by ropes which also attached it to the tent pole. In this primitive conveyance I was borne by eight Paharries homewards to Landour.

The jolting I underwent, and the stumps of trees that left their numerous prints on my back, brought me in a few hours into a state bordering on delirium. On descending the last valley before reaching Landour, a severer thump than usual caused me to start up, and bless my tormentors; the pole of the litter snapped, and away I rolled, with my dusky companions, towards the lower regions. The circular motion soon made me so giddy, that I might have rolled unconsciously into the next world, but my guardian angel interposed a little copse of bamboos between me and it. When I had recovered the senses remaining to me, and peered out of the copse to ascertain the locale of my fellow rollers, it was with feelings of mortification I counted and found all present and sound except one, who had luckily broken his nose.

Two hours after this event, I found myself in bed, contemplating the surgeon, as he tried the point of his lancet, with the feelings which a pig evidently possesses and betrays on perceiving the butcher sharpening his knife, preparatory to the final gash.

The fever was not unto death, as the reader (if there be such a person) will doubtless have concluded by the continuance of my narrative, and therefore as I cannot hope to excite much sympathy for my sufferings, or doubt as to the result, I had better recover at once, especially as that will occupy but a few words in the present instance, though it took me five weeks at that time.

I had scarcely recovered my strength after this attack, when news of a most warlike character arrived from the lower regions, inducing me to start immediately to rejoin my regiment, which it was rumoured was about to proceed immediately on active service. I reached Merut after two days' journey, and found all minds intent upon the approaching campaign in Scinde and Affghanistan.

I had not been many days in cantonments, before conjecture was changed to certainty, by the arrival of despatches from head quarters, ordering my regiment to form part of the army destined to assemble at Ferozepore on the Sutlej, about the latter end of November.

All now was bustle and business in our previously quiet cantonment. The furnace in the armourer's forge glowed with as much assiduity, and more brilliancy, doubtless, than that of yore at the shrine of the incomprehensible Vesta. On every side were heard the clicking of carbine and pistol locks; swords and lance-points sent sparkles of fire from countless grindstones, and above all other sounds rose the tumultuous din of the anvils.

CHAPTER III.

MATTERS RELATING TO THE AFGHANS—MARCH THROUGH DELHI TO FEROZEPORE—RUNJEET'S INTERVIEW—MARCH TOWARDS BUHAWULPORE.

THE circumstances on the north-western frontier, and beyond it, which caused these warlike preparations, were nearly as follow:—

The fortress of Herat, which formed the frontier bulwark of the kingdom of Caubul, but which was now in possession of Prince Kamran, (son of Mahmood, a deposed monarch of Afghanistan,) had been for some time invested by a large Persian force, instigated, it was imagined, by Russian influence. As this fortress opens a free ingress to the countries on our north-western frontier, the government of India felt particularly sensitive on its account, and suddenly commiserating its

VOL. I. D

forlorn condition, seized the present opportunity and pretext for advancing to its relief.

Shah Soojah Ool Moolk, having been deposed from the throne of Caubul, after the battle of Neemla, in 1809, had for many years been residing at Loodianah as a pensioner of the East India Company. At this juncture, the government of India, pitying the kingdomless state of that able monarch, resolved to reseat him on the throne, and thereby, and, in the accomplishment of that purpose, to further the following objects.

1st. The relief of the besieged fortress of Herat.

2ndly. The establishment of British supremacy and a military force in Afghanistan, as an outwork to obstruct any encroachments.

3rdly. The secure establishment of that long-meditated project, the navigation of the river Indus: the savage nations bordering thereon, with the exception of the Sikhs, having had but little intercourse with the British until Sir Alexander Burnes' memorable visit.

The throne of Caubul was at this time usurped by Dost Mahomed, brother of the late enterprising vizier, Futteh Khan, whose courage and abilities alone had retained the kingdom in the hands of the descendants of Ahmed Shah; until after the dethronement of Soojah, and murder of Mahmood, he transmitted it into more capable authority, the royal line having become equally obnoxious from imbecility, cowardice, and tyranny. Numerous factions, opposed to Dost Mahomed, still existed in Afghanistan, amongst the leaders of which, the most powerful were, Prince Kamran, the independent chief of Herat, and Dost Mahomed's own brothers, the Ameers of Candahar. There also existed considerable animosity between the members of rival families and tribes in Afghanistan, similar to those feuds which divided the clans of the Highlands even in the recent periods of Scottish history.

Sir Alexander Burnes had been resident for some time at the court of Dost Mahomed, but that monarch had latterly exhibited a decided Philo-Russian propensity, although, in the language of the East, he continued to profess himself the slave of the British: Burnes distrusted the royal sincerity, and had been recalled.

The fortress of Herat had been reduced to so weak a state, that apprehensions were daily entertained of its falling* a prey to the Persians,

---

* It must be borne in mind that forts are not carried by eastern nations with the celerity of modern art. A siege of two or three years' duration being a matter of frequent occurrence.

when an emissary from the British arrived with an offer of relief, which was joyfully accepted, and the defence of the city was carried on with renewed vigour, under the superintendence of Lieut. Pottinger, an officer of the East India Company's Engineers.

The Candahar chiefs, though suspected of being in communication with Persia, observed a strict neutrality in the present aspect of affairs.

Regarding the countries bordering on the Indus, no doubt was entertained of a ready compliance with the proposals of government, when accompanied by an argument of 20,000 well-disciplined troops.

The Punjaub, lying between the British frontier and Afghanistan, was at that time subject to the renowned Maharajah Runjeet Singh, between whom and the British power a well-observed alliance had existed for many years; but an insuperable religious hostility divided the Sikhs from the Afghans. Shah Soojah himself had experienced scanty clemency, when flying from his country through the Punjaub, after his defeat at Neemla, for he was seized by the old Lion of the Sikhs, thrown into prison, and robbed of every article he possessed, among which was the celebrated Koh-i-noor,* one of the most valuable jewels in existence. Shah Soojah having escaped from, or been let out of prison, as useless lumber, found a permanent refuge in the British territories.

A meeting was arranged to take place at Ferozepore between Runjeet Singh and the governor-general of India (Lord Auckland), at which the movements of the former, in co-operation with the British forces, were to be arranged.

Matters stood on the footing thus briefly described, when a portion of the Bengal army were ordered to assemble at Ferozepore, about the end of November, 1838 ; and, at the same time, a force from Bombay was directed to sail to the mouth of the Indus, and march along the banks of that river, meeting the Bengal army in the neighbourhood of Shikarpore.

At the latter end of October, the regiment to which I belonged marched out of cantonments, and encamped on the turf where many a spirited field day had been enacted during the previous season. On the following day our tents were all struck at the dawn of morning, and the

* "Koh-i-noor" means Mountain of Light, and is applied to a diamond something less than a pigeon's egg !

regiment marched about eight miles towards Delhi.

The fourth morning after leaving Meerut, we crossed the Jumna on a bridge of boats, and entered Delhi, the far-famed residence of the Mogul emperors ; formerly a city conspicuous for wealth and luxury, now equally so for the impudent demeanour of its inhabitants, the manufacture of shawls, and an intolerable abundance of flies.

Delhi still contains many substantial native residences, a vast extent of ruins in its suburbs, a few old tombs and mosques, the royal palace, and a thickly-peopled bazaar.

A high flight of steps at the end of one of the principal bazaars, leads to the mosque built by Shah Jehan, some two hundred years since. Passing under a narrow archway at the head of the steps, you enter a large square court, paved with stone. At the eastern side stands the high-domed praying-place, and each angle of the square is garnished with a lofty minaret, all built of red sandstone.

The court is edged with a low range of cloisters, over which is a battlemented terrace, commanding an extensive view of the city and suburbs.

In the distance is seen the celebrated Koutub—

a monument erected by an emperor of that name. This pillar is elegantly and elaborately carved, stands about two hundred and fifty feet in height, and is ascended by a spiral staircase.*

The original intention of the architect is unknown; the hieroglyphics supposed to convey important intelligence being a mystery; but it is conjectured that it must have been intended as a minaret for a projected mosque, which was never completed. Near the Koutub is a curious iron pillar, the intention of which is as much hidden in obscurity as that of the elegant minar. It appears to have irritated the destructive organ of Nadir Shah, who vainly endeavoured to dig it up, and failing in the experiment, brought his largest cannon to bear on the obnoxious pillar, which bears the impression of the ball, but stands as firmly as ever. We were informed that the mystery had recently been penetrated by a Brahmin sage, who had discovered that it was the axis of the earth: the principal objection to this ingenious theory perhaps consists in the latitude of this immovable pole.

* Koutub means, literally, the pole. The title of the emperor of that name was Koutub-ul-dien, or the pole-star of religion. He reigned at Lahore and Delhi, and died about A.D. 1210.

In the palace of the city still dwells the
nominal King of Delhi, the fallen representative
of the Mogul empire, now unable to command his
own movements—that is, if they should be directed to an escape from the courteous but actual
thraldom he undergoes. The palace is surrounded
by lofty battlemented walls of red granite, and a
deep moat. Passing through the ponderous gateway, you enter a large square court, whence
another archway leads into a second court, of
still greater dimensions, at the extremity of which
stands the audience hall, built on eight massive
pillars of alabaster. In the centre of this hall
stands a throne of pure crystal, on which, our
native guide informed us, had sat many a mighty
emperor. " See, then, a mightier than the present king of the Mogul empire sit on that
throne," exclaimed one of our officers, bringing
himself to an anchor on the tempting seat. The
amazed guide turned up his eyes in pious horror,
expecting the apparition of some monarch of that
mighty line to avenge this invasion of his royal
seat of honour; but they seemed disposed to put
up with the affront, or perhaps to acquiesce in the
observation, and remained quiet in their graves.

From hence we passed into the palace gardens,
on the Jumna's banks, which were once the ad-

miration of all beholders, but now much neglected.

Here I observed, under an alcove, a sickly-looking lad, who proved to be the king's eldest son, and heir-apparent, amusing himself with lighting crackers, and pelting them at his attendants, or thrusting them in the faces of those he could reach—a pretty fair emblem of what the petty tyrant might become were time and opportunity afforded him. Yet, even in modern times, have men raised an incubus of this class to oppress and torture themselves, and, bending meekly to the royal idol, earned and deserved the infliction. The recent history of India, not a century ago, teems with instances which cast far in the shade the comparatively feeble efforts of Domitian or Commodus.

The cholera was raging to an awful extent whilst we were encamped outside the walls of Delhi, and upwards of two hundred were daily falling victims. Though we felt not the scourge at once, the column had not proceeded many marches before the seeds of the disease, probably brought from hence, and lurking among us, burst and spread devastation around.

The experimental camel-battery, in charge of Major Pew, joined our brigade, which had been formed at Delhi, and accompanied us to Ferozepore.

On the 4th of November we quitted Delhi, and marched through an uninteresting country, overspread with low jungle and marsh, save where a small village, perched on an eminence, enlivened the view by the cultivation in its neighbourhood. A chain of pickets was now posted daily, and an officer sent about twenty miles in advance to explore and report on the country to our brigadier.

The cholera, that scourge of the east, now made its appearance amongst us, carrying off three of our men the first day, and sending numbers into hospital, but singularly enough not another fell a victim to the disease, which confined itself to the natives and committed dire havoc amongst them. Numbers died on the line of march daily, and the camp and hospital were literally strewn with dead bodies.

No sooner had the pestilence stricken them than they succumbed to fate without using an effort to obtain relief, and died often without a struggle in less than an hour after their seizure.

Grass-cutters, coolies, and the lower castes, were the principal victims, and few were the officers in camp who had not to lament the loss of some servants carried off during the four days the epidemic resided with us.

The causes assigned, by the medical men, for

the outbreak of cholera, were the unripe grain used by the natives as food, and the rank vegetation springing around us ; for we were passing still through jungle, interwoven with long coarse grass. However, this continued the same the whole way to Ferozepore nearly, and the scourge remained but four days upon us, which does not tend to strengthen the above mentioned reason. I know not why we should attempt to assign causes for the prevalence of cholera, whilst those of many other diseases are unheeded.

One learned practitioner (a Dr. Tytler) has written a book to prove that the malady is caused by the prevalent use of rice amongst the natives of India, and proposes calling the cholera the "Morbus Oryzeus." No doubt the change of name was in order to show the choleric imp how well we knew him, and to warn him off.

But, however applicable the theory might seem to India, the learned doctor must find some other reason for its European visit, where rice is certainly not the principal food of the inhabitants. To those acquiescing in the Tytler theory, I can only recommend, in the words of Horace,

"Spectatum admissi *risum* teneatis amici."

On the 28th of November we reached Ferozepore, the general rendevous for the Bengal force, and found the army encamped about four miles from the left bank of the Sutlej.

Lord Auckland and Sir Henry Fane had also arrived, to meet Runjeet Singh, who was encamped, with a force of 20,000 troops, on the opposite bank, and had thrown a bridge of boats across the river. The Sutlej was then about two hundred and fifty yards in breadth, rolling sluggishly over its muddy bed, and through a country where little was to be seen but long dry grass and low jhow jungle.

The town was undergoing considerable improvements, under the hands of our engineers. The fort, too, was re-echoing to the mason's and carpenter's weapons, and most of the narrow streets in the suburbs were being levelled, to make way for a wide and massive bazaar, so that, from a mean and dirty place, Ferozepore bids fair to become, ere long, a large and flourishing town.

The army, daily arriving, were encamped northwest of Ferozepore, between it and the Sutlej, and consisted of—

The Cavalry Brigade, commanded by Colonel Arnold, comprising Her Majesty's 16th Lancers, 2nd and 3rd Native Cavalry, and one troop Horse Artillery.

1st Infantry Brigade, commanded by Colonel Sale: of Her Majesty's 13th Light Infantry, two regiments Native Infantry, and the Camel Battery.

2nd Infantry Brigade, Colonel Dennis: Her Majesty's 3rd Buffs, two regiments Native Infantry, Sappers.

3rd Infantry Brigade, Colonel Roberts: Company's European regiment, two regiments Native Infantry, Park of Artillery.

4th Brigade, Colonel Nott: three regiments Native Infantry.

5th Brigade, Colonel Paul: three regiments Native Infantry, one company Artillery, besides engineers, commissariat, and staff.

The day after our arrival, Maharajah Runjeet Singh came over to visit Lord Auckland, and I accompanied the governor-general's escort on the occasion. After remaining upwards of six hours in the saddle, in front of Lord Auckland's Durbar tents, we heard the welcome sound of Runjeet's gongs and nousheras approaching, and shortly after, from beneath a massive canopy of dust, emerged the motley array of Runjeet's elephants and cavalcade. Now, hundreds of gaily clad Sikh horsemen—some in bright chain armour, others in various coloured silks and cloth of gold, brandished their long spears, flung back their brass embossed shields, and galloped with headlong fury around the maharajah's elephants, exhibiting to us the singular dexterity with which they could wield their arms and manage their horses.

As the procession approached, Runjeet was conspicuous in front, on an enormous elephant, and dressed in a plain suit of ruby coloured cashmere, with a turban of the same colour, whilst on his arm glittered the famous koh-i-noor, the diamond which, as I before mentioned, his highness obtained in no very creditable manner from Shah Soojah.

The maharajah was rather below the middling stature, slight in form, and his face expressive of the shrewdest cunning. The leer that occasionally escaped from his single optic seemed to tell a clear tale of debauchery. He was then about fifty-six years of age, although I should have taken him to be more; but an unbridled devotion to ardent spirits tells on personal appearance, and appeared to have corroded his iron frame.

After the chief had passed, a swarm of Sikhs

followed, some on horseback and some on foot, dressed in the most fantastical and grotesque style, but at the same time the materials were generally of a costly and extravagant quality. The long spear and matchlock appeared to be their favourite weapons; but many were armed only with tolwars and daggers. The rear was closed up by a battalion of infantry, dressed much like our sepoys, and drilled according to the French system of military tactics, introduced by General Alard.

As Runjeet approached the audience tent, Lord Auckland and Sir Henry Fane put their elephants in motion to meet him, and, after sundry greetings and salaams, the whole party proceeded to the Durbar, where the principal actors were obscured from our view by the dense mass of British officers and Sikhs, who thronged in after them. What passed is barely worthy of record. Lord Auckland presented a picture of Queen Victoria, which Runjeet, with becoming gallantry, pressed to his lips. After sundry professions of inviolable friendship, Runjeet made some inquiries regarding Aden, which Sir Henry Fane informed him was occupied by a British garrison. In a short time they adjourned to look at some cannon, which had been brought as a present to the maharajah, and over which both he and Sir Henry narrowly escaped breaking their heads, having stumbled on a heap of cannon balls arranged near the tent.

Accompanied by his suite, Runjeet remounted his elephant amidst a deafening salute from the guns of the camel-battery; these seemed to take his fancy vastly; and, drawing up opposite them, he saw the camels yoked and the guns drawn past him, expressing great delight and astonishment at the neatness and regularity of this newly constructed battery.

When the maharajah had departed, we also returned to camp, which we did not reach before one o'clock, when the sun, although a December one, was fiercely hot.

On the 1st of December, Lord Auckland returned Runjeet's visit. We arrived at the river about sunrise, and having crossed on the bridge of boats, found Runjeet's army drawn up, and forming a street from the river to the Durbar tents. Nearest to us were the cavalry, the same motley hordes we had seen two days before; beyond them, stood the infantry, dressed, both in the military and common acceptation of the term, with extraordinary attention; and if they will fight as well as they look, are likely to do their master good service. Next came a body of goor-cheras, or irregular horsemen, dressed in white, and armed with lances and matchlocks—a remarkably fine-looking body of men, but generally believed to have an insuperable objection to injure their fellow-creatures. Much as we may admire their philanthropy, we must nevertheless admit the quality to be objectionable in a military point of view. In rear of this array of philanthropists, were disposed a numerous body of surwars, mounted on camels, and carrying swivel-guns, which looked like large blunderbusses, from which abominable instruments an incessant firing was kept up from the time we crossed the river until we recrossed on our return.

The governor-general having made his appearance in the street of Sikhs, Runjeet and his court advanced at a rapid pace on their elephants to greet his excellency. The dust arose in such masses as for a time obscured every object; but at the point of junction of the two parties, the concentrated cloud slowly drifted aside, and displayed to our dazzled sight the richest blaze of Eastern splendour that for many years had reflected the rays of our destructive enemy.

The elephants' housings in Runjeet's suite were made of gorgeously-embroidered gold cloth, and surmounted by howdahs, inlaid with ivory and ebony; and Runjeet and his attendants, glittering with silver and gold, silks and precious stones, formed a marked contrast to the governor-general and his retinue in their scarlet or blue uniforms.

The maharajah, as before, was remarkable among the Sikh throng for the uniformity of his costume, and the noble elephant which carried him, on which Lord Auckland had now seated himself, at Runjeet's invitation; and the whole procession moved rapidly towards the Durbar tents.

Disengaging myself from the mêlée which ensued, I galloped up the street, and after some difficulty, succeeded in effecting an entrance through the silken gateway. Within, was a garden, where the rarest evergreens and flowers were growing, having sprung up, as if by magic,* during the night. In the centre, was the Durbar-tent, made of strongly-woven Cashmere, and supported by silver poles. The floor was spread with Persian carpets, and the furniture was of frosted silver, inlaid with golden ornaments.

The maharajah having seated himself, Sir

* This *magic* garden had been imported from Lahore, and planted during the night.

Henry Fane and Lord Auckland took their places on each side.

Behind Runjeet stood his prime minister, the wily and tyrannous Dhian Singh, clad in a panoply of bright steel armour, elaborately gilded. Little could be seen of his face besides the dark flashing eyes and high-bridged nose, for a monstrous pair of moustaches and a beard covered his visage and a great part of his body also.

A glittering string of diamonds and emeralds encircled his neck; and in his turban stood a bustard's feather, fastened by a diamond brooch. Scattered about the tent were many of the sirdars and ministers, remarkable, principally, for the variety and magnificence of their attire and the length of their beards.

Mr. Macnaghten, who had been appointed British envoy to Caubul in the meditated operations, stood in front of the trio, acting as interpreter on the occasion, during which I did not hear any political subject discussed.

Runjeet, finding matters look heavy and irksome, sent for a party of Punjaubee girls, to dance and sing for the amusement of his two solemn visitors. The young ladies who made their appearance were not remarkable for beauty : amongst the whole coterie, I saw but two girls who could be called pretty. I did not hear, and lament I cannot record, the opinions of the governor-general and commander-in-chief on this particular.

The imposing ballet being ended, and the little Nautch damsels having filed off, presents of Cashmere shawls and jewellery were brought on trays and exhibited. When these had been taken away, there seemed no chance of any more amusements. Poor Runjeet's stock was exhausted; he looked dreadfully ennuyé; and it certainly seemed a relief to the chief performers when the party broke up. We all hastened to get back to our posts when the ceremony was over, though much impeded by the inquisitiveness of the Sikhs, whose curiosity about every trifle was quite insatiable. A long-haired barbarian begged to be informed the use of a sabretash, which seemed to take his fancy much, and inquired if it was used to carry provisions? He was informed that we seldom or ever touched food for many days on a campaign if there were much hard fighting. "Wau, wau!" exclaimed the astonished barbarian, dropping the sabretash, and gazing in his informant's face with equal amazement and credulity.

A Sikh sipahee, remarking some British officers with few symptoms of manhood visible on their faces, quaintly inquired what rank those young ladies held in the army!

Benighted savage! he little knew, and perhaps could never understand, the absolute and tyrannous sway maintained by our Northern fair!

About mid-day, we recrossed the bridge of boats, and returned, under a scorching sun, to camp.

The following day, a review of the British forces was held, for the benefit of the maharajah. About ten thousand men were under arms at daybreak; but from that time till noon, when we returned to camp, everything was wrapped in an almost impenetrable veil of dust.

The next day, Runjeet gave us a field-day on his side of the river, which I was prevented by duty from witnessing; but from the picket near the Sutlej, where I was posted, the firing of the infantry and artillery seemed quite as rapid, though not quite so steady, as our own. Indeed, most of the officers returned astonished to find the Sikh army so effective and well-disciplined.

For this discipline, Runjeet was mainly indebted to Generals Alard and Ventura, two officers of the French imperial army, who passed through Lahore on their travels from Persia to Hindostan. They were detained by Runjeet in a sort of honorary captivity, until he succeeded in inducing them to enter his service. At the expiration of six months, Ventura exhibited to the maharajah a battalion of Sikhs, organized on the French system of military tactics, and Runjeet, as may be supposed, was greatly pleased at the incalculable improvement in his men's appearance.

One circumstance gave considerable annoyance to the sensitive general, which was the indomitable taste for finery among the subordinate officers, many of whom far surpassed their commander in richness of costume. This circumstance was turned to some account by the politic Ventura, who insinuated to his master that many officers of his battalion were enabled to wear richer lace and bullion than he could procure or afford. Runjeet replied, that he would put it beyond their power to do so any longer, and caused to be made and presented to Ventura a pair of pearl epaulettes of unrivalled magnificence.

Both these officers remained long in the service of the Sikhs. Alard died shortly before the old Lion himself, but Ventura remained to serve his successor Shere Singh.

A continual scene of festivity prevailed in Runjeet's camp during our halt at Ferozepore. The sound of music and revelry was borne on the evening breeze, the rattle of feu-de-joie rang daily in our ears, and at night the welkin glowed with fire-works and illuminations.

At length, the order for our march was issued, and the proclamation stated, that in consequence of recent intelligence* from Herat, the commander-in-chief, and governor-general deemed it requisite to prosecute the campaign with the following troops only—viz.,

The Cavalry Brigade, and Camel Battery.

Three Brigades of Infantry and the Artillery of the Park, with two troops of Horse Artillery.

The whole Bengal force was placed under command of Sir Willoughby Cotton, until its junction with the Bombay army, when Sir John Keane was to assume command of the united forces, as Sir Henry Fane was suffering severely from ill health, and about to resign his command and return to England.

Colonel Thackwell, of the 3rd Light Dragoons, was appointed to command the cavalry division, consisting of two brigades, one from the Bengal, the other from the Bombay presidency.

On the tenth of December, we commenced our march from Ferozepore, passing, during the first

* Viz., the news then received of the Persians having retired from Herat.

four days, through the protected Sikh states, and encamping near villages where supplies were abundant and water excellent.

On the fifth day, we entered the territories of Bahawul Khan, concerniug whom many false reports had been prevalent in camp, setting forth his ill disposition towards the British, and his desire to impede our progress through his country; the propagators of these fanciful rumours fathering them invariably on the most plausible and least tangible authorities.

The confidential whispers of the envoy who was in our rear, or of Sir Alexander Burnes, who was in advance, were usually quoted by these alarmists to command attention to their fabrications. At first, these tales formed matter of amusement and speculation on the line of march; but as falsehoods were daily multiplied, the authors, and their inventions, became a fair subject of ridicule, and, as in the fable of the shepherd's boy and the wolf, all reports were alike disbelieved. However, the information department, during the whole campaign, was not eminently successful; and this may, in some degree, palliate the superabundance of false reports prevalent during the whole march, which, in many instances, had influence over those in command, and were productive of mischievous results.

During our march through the Bahawulpore country, we found an abundant stock of grain collected for us at each encampment, which enabled the commissariat to reserve the stores laid in for the campaign.

During each morning's march, the Sutlej lay about two or three miles distant. The country adjacent to it was well cultivated, and in some places covered with thick underwood; yet, notwithstanding the abundant supply of fuel on the river's banks, many commissariat camels had been laden with wood for the use of the army, which had much more need of grain and other useful stores, of which ere long they bitterly felt the want. It is worthy of observation, that Burnes, in his report of the Indus and Sutlej, made frequent mention of the jungle in their vicinity.

Although the prospect, thus far, was sufficiently cheering on the right, that on our left flank presented a dreary contrast. We had reached the borders of that extensive desert which lies south and east of Bahawulpore, and reduces the cultivated tract of this country to a mere strip of land, bordering the Sutlej. Far as the eye could reach when turned towards the British possessions, nothing was discernible but a barren and track-less desert. Here and there, a few hillocks had collected and risen over some untimely shrubs, which had sprung up unconscious of their fatal position, until the domineering sands, jealous of such an encroachment on their demesnes, arose and entombed their helpless victims, leaving these mounds as so many trophies to assert their resist-less and desolating sway.

The roads were deep and sandy, causing the artillery horses and bullocks severe labour in dragging the guns. But the camels of Major Pew's battery were quite in their element on the desert, and stalked lustily away with the heavy guns and carriages.

About the end of December, we had some light showers of rain, which rendered the climate delightfully cool in the day-time, (the nights and mornings had been piercingly cold for some weeks,) and cloth garments were in great requi-sition.

The inhabitants of the country were so peace-ably disposed, that we were enabled to send on tents over night according to the custom in India, which ensures, on arrival in camp, every morning, the luxuries of a cup of coffee, a couch, and a bath; the latter is taken *al fresco* from a skin filled with water, and poured over the shoulders by a native. Notwithstanding the good feeling exhibited by the country-people, our military authorities seemed resolved to distrust them, and posted a squadron on picket, day and night, with orders to keep mounted patrols on the alert. An opportunity was hereby afforded of exercising our vigilance on the camel-drivers and grass-cutters near the camp, and also of ascertaining by experiment, how much deterioration would be effected in the constitution of man and horse, by a curtailment of natural rest, added to long daily marches, and what length of time would be required to effect that object: the result amply solved the problem.

The jungle, on the banks of the river, held a vast quantity of game; the most numerous of which, was the black partridge—a bird also found in many parts of Hindostan, and the most beautifully marked, I think, of the feathered tribe. They frequent the jhow* jungle during the heat of the day, and require an extensive and compact line of beaters to get them out of the thick covert. Hare, snipe, and quail, were also plentiful, and, occasionally, we met with a great variety of wild duck and water-fowl of almost every description, among

* The jhow is a shrub resembling the yew tree, and affords good food for the camels.

the marshes by the river side. The shooting in these marshes can only be followed by those who despise malaria, for they are proverbially unhealthy : the excitement of meeting a stray tiger, or sinking in one of the treacherous quicksands which abound in the vicinity of the Sutlej, and are generally felt before they are seen, may add zest to more adventurous sportsmen.

The distance from Ferozepore to Bahawulpore was two hundred and twenty-one miles, according to our route; this, we overcame in eighteen marches, having halted twice for a day. The government agents had been exerting themselves to get supplies laid in for us at each march, but complaints were urged against Bahawul Khan, of not having duly exerted himself in forwarding this object. Poor man ! no doubt he entertained strong fear regarding his own independence, after the military visit with which he was now threatened—no British troops having marched this road previously. Shah Soojah, with his motley contingent,* preceded the column, and no doubt seized the lion's share of whatever supplies he met with, and from his previous character, there

---

* This contingent consisted of raw Hindoo levies raised for Shah Soojah's guard, in Afghanistan, amounting to about five thousand men and four guns.

is no reason to suppose that Bahawul Khan entertained a high opinion of our royal companion.

Our army now marched in five columns, the sappers and miners in advance, the cavalry-brigade next, and the three infantry-brigades in succession, at intervals of one day's march between each brigade.

CHAPTER IV.

ARRIVAL AT BAHAWULPORE — SIR HENRY FANE'S INTER-
VIEW WITH THE KHAN — PROGRESS TO SCINDE ACROSS
THE INDUS.

On the 29th of December, the cavalry-brigade reached Bahawulpore, in the vicinity of which the country is richly cultivated. The view was enlivened by hordes of Bahawul Khan's wild-looking cavalry, encamped amongst the groves of palm and date trees in the neighbourhood.

We marched into our camp near the city under a heavy fall of rain, and were met by a son of the khan, who came to pay his respects to Sir Willoughby Cotton, whilst his father visited Sir Henry Fane on board his boats, which kept parallel with the army during its progress.

On the 31st, Sir Henry returned the visit, attended by a numerous suite of officers. Bahawul

Khan made no efforts to display any splendour; perhaps, he considered it politic to affect poverty in the presence of the British chief. The conversation was as interesting as usual on the like occasions, and ran, as well as I can remember, nearly as follows : —

SIR HENRY.—I come as the emissary of the British government, to offer you their friendship.

B. KHAN.—I am sensible of the condescension displayed towards me, both by them and yourself, in granting this interview.

SIR HENRY.—The British government are just and equitable, faithful to their friends, terrible to their enemies, (looking very dignified, and rather fierce.)

B. KHAN.—I fully appreciate the magnitude of the British name, and see their power. All I have is theirs, and I am your slave.

SIR HENRY.—Now, talk we of other matters. Is not the climate unusually cold for this season of the year, at Bahawulpore ?

B. KHAN.—It is, undoubtedly ; but at the present moment, I feel neither cold nor damp, whilst basking in the sunshine of your presence.

Sir Henry was looking blue with cold, and stiff with dignity ; so the khan must have been of a fiery temperament if he spoke the truth.

Such was the substance of the conversation that passed between the two potentates; but setting bombast aside, Bahawul Khan has always expressed to those officers who visited his capital the utmost respect for the British, and an anxiety to preserve a sincere alliance. His decision has been unquestionably politic; for, by placing himself under British protection, he has saved his country from the rapacity of his formidable neighbours, the Sikhs.

The city of Bahawulpore is of considerable extent, and surrounded by a dilapidated mud wall, about twelve feet in height and four in thickness. The principal houses are built of brick, but huddled so closely together, as to engender filth and heat to an unnecessary degree. The khan's palace is in the centre of the town, and presents as mean an exterior as the other houses. Of the interior, I can form no estimate, not having visited it. The narrow bazaars were thronged all day; and trade seemed to be flourishing briskly amongst the twenty thousand inhabitants which Bahawulpore is said to contain.

Woollens, hardware, and a variety of fruit, seemed to be the principal articles exposed for sale; but the prevalent commodity is undoubtedly filth.

The men are certainly a larger, better looking, and more brawny race than that of the upper provinces of Bengal.

The women are so carefully wrapped in veils, that I was enabled to catch only a faint glimpse of their faces, and a very indistinct one of their figures; but the damsels of the East usually evince greater anxiety to conceal their face than any other part of their persons.

The only Bahawulpore fair ones I had a good opportunity of seeing and speaking to, were some dancing-girls, attending the khan's party, whilst in our camp. They were lively creatures, with very fair skins, laughing black eyes, and the airy, graceful figures that are almost the universal characteristic of Eastern belles.

The city is about three miles distant from the Sutlej, which must ere long be the grand channel of communication between the upper provinces of Bengal and the Bombay presidency. Its turbid surface, now seldom unruffled by aught save the occasional plunge of a startled alligator, will soon resound to the cries of busy boatmen and the plash of innumerable oars.

On New Year's day, 1839, we resumed our march, bidding adieu to the Sutlej, which diverges hence a little to the west, and unites its waters

E 3

with the Chinab, which, thirty miles below this confluence, falls into the Indus.

As we advanced, the desert continued on our left, cheerless as ever; but at every ten or twelve miles, we found a halting-place at some village, near which were usually some fields of grain, and invariably good water.

The stunted shrubs continued to afford us ample firewood, and the occasional hamlets grain enough to feed our horses without indenting on the commissariat stores.

Khanpore, eight marches from Bahawulpore, is a city of considerable extent, and occasionally the residence of Bahawul Khan, who visits it on account of the abundance of wild boar and hog deer frequenting the neighbouring jungles, many of which we saw in our shooting-excursions, and occasionally on the line of march.

The governor fired a royal salute as the cavalry-brigade marched through the city, which compliment was cheaply returned (ammunition being valuable) by our band striking up " God save the king !"—who the monarchs were, to whom these royal honours were paid, we were unable to ascertain.

Here, many of our servants and camp-followers deserted during the night; nor were we able to recover any of the runaways. There is a track from hence to Hissar, across the desert, which they probably took, being weary of the long march, and frightened by the account of some fruit-merchants from Caubul, in camp, who expatiated on the cold of Afghanistan and the ferocity of its inhabitants.

Five marches beyond this place, brought us to the frontiers of the Ameers of Scinde, where we were joined by Sir Alexander Burnes, who seemed dubious of the peaceful disposition of the Hydrabad Ameers, though their cousin of Khyrpoor professed his readiness to co-operate in the free navigation of the Indus.

This part of Upper Scinde is overgrown with thick jungle, which is cleared in the neighbourhood of villages, to make room for crops of jewar, coarse sugar-cane, and wheat. The natives seem a hardy and industrious race; but the tribes of Beloochees, from the mountains on the right bank of the Indus, infest the country, and are its bane, exercising a despotic authority over the unfortunate and peaceable Scindians, and plundering travellers and merchants of all countries who venture this road without a sufficient protection. No sooner had we crossed the boundary-line, than we were cautioned not to venture singly any distance from camp, as these marauders were sure to be hovering in the vicinity, on the look-out for plunder; and several camp-followers were daily murdered by these savages for the sake of the few pieces of silver in their possession, or, failing these, for the clothes they wore ; yet in spite of these numerous examples, the roving propensities of our followers were not easily overcome.

Hitherto, no communication had been received from Sir John Keane, who was to land at Kurachee, one of the mouths of the Indus, and advance by the right bank of the river to Shikarpore, having previously arranged the terms of a treaty with the Ameers of Hydrabad, either amicably or with the bayonet.

When we had arrived within three marches of Bukkur Island and fort, where it was intended that the army should cross the Indus, intelligence was received from Sir John Keane, announcing his arrival at Tatta, a large town on the right bank, about forty miles below Hydrabad;[*] he had experienced great difficulties even in reaching that place, from want of carriage, and the unfriendly disposition of the Ameers.

---

[*] Sir J. Keane's forces were about three thousand five hundred men, and thirty guns.

Hydrabad was fortified in the usual native fashion, and was said to be garrisoned by more than twenty thousand Beloochees: confiding in these troops, (or, at their dictation,) the Ameer had rejected the terms proposed by the political agent, Colonel Pottinger, which were—

1st. The payment of thirty lakhs of rupees, the arrears of tribute due to Shah Soojah.

2ndly. To throw open, and promote by every means in their power, the free navigation of the Indus.

3rdly. To support a force of four thousand troops to be quartered in Scinde.

It appeared far from surprising that the Ameers, who had always been noted for a jealousy of intercourse with strangers, and especially with the British, should have felt averse to comply with terms which rendered Scinde, at one stroke of the pen, a mere dependency on our colossal Eastern empire.

On the march towards Bukkur, the jungle was so thick on each side of the road, that the Scindians, had they been disposed to annoy us, had many opportunities of effecting that object almost with impunity. One morning, about daybreak, the advanced guard missed the road, and led nearly the whole army astray in the woods, where the paths branching in many directions, induced each party to wander according to their fancy. Col. Ninny, an officer of remarkable intelligence, who accompanied the party with which I was wandering, pushed resolutely forward, insisting that the path he followed must be the right one. " But surely, sir," remonstrated one of the officers, " this cannot be the way, for we now face the rising sun, and our proper direction is nearly west." The intellectual features of the gallant colonel were contracted with ineffable scorn, as he replied, " And pray, sir, what has the sun got to do with our road?"

Though blind at the time to the acuteness of the observation, I have since dwelt upon it, as singularly characteristic of that gifted individual, who, with a steady perseverance, has braved obstacles, which, (as in the present case,) judged by the fallacious test of reason, would have appeared to ordinary men insuperable! Unhappily, in this instance, the combinations of that *great mind* were not allowed time for development, as an aide-de-camp rode up, and pointing to the rear, indicated that the road lay in that direction, and the general would be happy to see us on it.

On the morning of the 25th of January we

marched up to the town of Rohree and encamped on the banks of the Indus.

Rohree is built on a flinty rock that rises abruptly on the left side of the river, which had hitherto been low and full of dangerous quicksands. A range of bare hills, trending to the south, run from Rohree, throughout lower Scinde, and terminate in the Delta, a few miles from the sea. From the southern part of the town, a thick grove of bastard date-trees extends many miles along the river's banks, adding considerably to the beauty of the view. In the river, opposite to Rohree, and between it and Sukkur, stands the important island and fortress of Bukkur. The site is low and sandy, but the fort, which is built of brick, stands about thirty feet in height, and is commanded from either bank, as the Indus is less than eight hundred yards in breadth at this season.

From Sukkur, on the opposite shore, the bank rises to a considerable elevation, opposing a barrier to the encroachment of the waters at the periods of inundation. On the left shore, the whole country is intersected by watercourses, made for the purpose of retaining the water after the inundation, which is said to cover a large extent of country.

A few miles from Rohree are the ruins of the ancient city of Alore, which present to the view an extensive field of devastation. They afford little interest to the traveller, as the few edifices standing are so dilapidated, and the imagery so nearly effaced, as to baffle the researches of the most patient antiquarian. The indefatigable Burnes has pursued the subject with his usual intelligence, but such matters afford more scope for conjecture than research, as the earlier periods of Indian history are deeply involved in darkness and fable. We were, however, informed by a learned aide-de-camp of the commander-in-chief, that Alexander the Great had halted there for two days, and he even indicated the position of the royal pavilion with as much confidence as if he had been present on the occasion, which placed the question beyond a doubt.

The river was now a scene of much activity, the chief engineer being engaged in collecting boats to form a bridge to Sukkur, which required a numerous assemblage, the distance to Bukkur island being nearly 400 yards, though beyond it the channel was very narrow.

Ameer Roostum Khan, to whom this part of Scinde belonged, was residing at Khyrpore, about fifteen miles from Rohree, and came into camp the day after our arrival, to visit the commander-in-chief. The treaty above mentioned was shown to him, and he laid it on his head in token of obedience. The hostile disposition of his relatives at Hydrabad being alluded to, he urged the improbability of their offering any resistance, and entreated permission to negotiate with them.

Sir Henry Fane replied that the day for any mediation had passed, and broke up the Durbar, by inviting the Ameer to ride with him and see the troops, which would march the following day towards Hydrabad, to co-operate with Sir John Keane in enforcing the terms proposed.

Meer Roostum, mounting his horse, accompanied Sir Henry along the line, appearing far from at his ease whilst inspecting the display of force which reduced him to a vassal, and was intended to operate against his kinsmen.

Arrangements were then made for the cession of Bukkur island fort, to be garrisoned by a British force, which he assented to with great reluctance, but it was then too late to raise objections, as the net for Scinde was cast, and he had become entangled in its meshes. The second and third day, however, passed without any intimation being given that the fort was at our service, and the force intended for Hydrabad having been delayed in consequence, Sir Henry resolved to wait no longer. On the evening of the 30th, a sepoy regiment, accompanied by Sir Willoughby Cotton, embarked from Rohree, to occupy Bukkur, and two guns were posted above the town to command the fort in case of resistance.

The squadron to which I belonged was that evening on picket near the town, from whence we had a favourable position for observing the operations of this memorable siege. The boats were off, and we now fancied we saw the garrison training a large gun on the walls to bear against the fleet. All stood in breathless expectation for the signal which would, in all probability, kindle far and wide the devastating flames of war.

The troops now reached the island, and as yet no shot had been fired; admittance was demanded, and no answer returned. Sir Willoughby ordered a skin filled with powder to be attached to the gate and fired, and whilst a party were in the act of obeying this order, the portals were suddenly thrown open, and we observed the garrison, amounting perhaps to *twenty* in number, not in the act of levelling their matchlocks at the intruders, but more prudently sallying from a side postern, and quietly dropping down the river towards Hydrabad.

The transition was so sudden and absurd, that a general burst of laughter issued from the spectators at sight of the formidable garrison, which was expected to make so daring a resistance.

That evening the fort was occupied by a regiment of native infantry, and before the sun went down we beheld the British flag slowly unfold itself to the evening breeze, and float for the first time in authority over the waters of the majestic Indus.

Early next morning, the cavalry, artillery, and first brigade of infantry, under Colonel Sale, commenced their march towards Hydrabad. Accounts were rife in camp that a force of six or seven thousand Beloochees were lying in ambush to attack us on the march, or fall on our camp during the night, and therefore the cavalry threw out parties in advance to feel for these hidden savages. For the first six miles, we marched in a thick grove of bastard date trees, the road through which was flanked by mud walls about six feet high—a glorious chance for the Beloochee tirailleurs, which they unwisely neglected. Emerging from this grove, we entered a well-cultivated, though woody country, and plainly discovered the traces of a camp broken up that morning. The force (whatever it might have been) were no doubt retreating before us upon Hydrabad.

Accounts were this day received that Sir John Keane had been detained some days at Jerrikh, two marches from Hydrabad, but had arrived at Kotra, on the right bank of the Indus, and nearly opposite Hydrabad. The following day, native reports reached us that the Beloochees had floated across the Indus on rafts supported on Kedgeree pots,* and routed the British forces; but we unanimously concluded that the Ameers were on far too bad terms with his excellency to think of crossing the river and taking such *pot luck* with the British.

Shah Soojah, who had reached Shikarpore, with his contingent, some days before our arrival at Rohree, was now marching on the right bank of the Indus towards Larkhana, which place (a city of the Hydrabad Ameers) he occupied with little resistance.

No baggage being allowed to precede our column on the line of march, and the weather becoming exceedingly hot, we suffered severely from the heat before our tents came up, which

* A common way of crossing rivers in the East, the pots being bound together by a framework of bamboo.

they rarely did before mid-day, and on a long march not till considerably later.

The soil in this district is fertile and well cultivated, and the population must be considerable, judging from the numerous well-inhabited villages we passed, where the natives regarded us in a friendly light, and brought abundance of supplies into camp. The rule of the Ameers is far from popular amongst the Scindians; and the tribes of marauding Beloochees, whom the Ameers confessed their inability to restrain, are of course viewed with horror by the peaceful agriculturists, who therefore hailed us in the light of deliverers. Their intercourse with our camp-followers, who, having long worn the collar, were no doubt willing to see it encircle strange necks also, tended to encourage this amicable disposition.

The fifth march from Rohree, we closed with the river near Noona Goth, where the lower range of the Hala mountains were distinctly seen, trending, apparently, in a direct line towards the Indus. These mountains, the Scindians told us, were about forty miles distant. The seventh march, we reached Kanjaree, a frontier town of the Hydrabad district, where, in the course of the morning, a courier arrived from Sir J. Keane, announcing the submission of the Hydrabad

Ameers. They had held out, it appeared, until the appearance of the British forces on the bank of the river opposite the capital, when, after frequent unsuccessful negotiations, a treaty was at length concluded by Colonel Pottinger, with the modification that no British troops should be quartered in Hydrabad. In signing this treaty, the Ameers declared they were acting in opposition to the wishes of their soldiery, and that in doing so they sealed irrevocably their own doom.

Thus ended our chance of a golden harvest in Hydrabad, then known to be one of the richest cities of the East; the policy which saved it for a few years ended in annexing the lands to the British possessions, and in consigning the rulers to captivity: but the merits of this subject now form a matter of debate between two of the most gallant and accomplished soldiers of the age, Sir C. Napier and Colonel Outram.

We now turned our heads and thoughts towards Afghanistan with a pleasanter prospect for the ensuing summer than that of passing it under canvas in Scinde, which is notoriously one of the hottest and most unhealthy parts of the world.*

* The reserve force from Bombay, which occupied Scinde soon after our departure, (amounting to about three thousand men,) bore witness to its qualities in both respects.

We reached Rohree in a week, retracing the route by which we had advanced, and found that the bridge of boats across the Indus had been completed, and that the part of our force which had remained behind at Rohree, commenced the transit on the 14th of February.

Having halted three days, we crossed the river at sunrise in single files, dismounted, and leading our horses, such being deemed the safest method. The passage was effected without a single accident, even to the baggage. The bridge was firmly constructed, and well moored, reflecting credit on Captain Thompson, of the Bengal engineers, under whose direction it had been formed. The stream near the left bank ran with great velocity; but as we approached Bukkur Island, there was little or none; beyond the fort, the bridge was scarcely a hundred yards in length, and the current very weak. Four hundred and ninety yards were mentioned, in general orders, as the distance bridged; but the portion of the island we crossed must have been upwards of two hundred and fifty yards in breadth.

We now, for the first time, marched in rear of the army; and on our arrival at Shikarpore, found the whole force, including Shah Soojah and his new levies, encamped round the city.

Shikarpore stands in a barren and desolate-looking plain, which well assorts with the white and mouldering mud walls surrounding the place. This was the general depôt of supplies for the army; but in lieu of the commodious and well-stocked shops we had expected to see, we found the bazaar little superior to Bahawulpore, or even Rohree, except being somewhat larger and more thronged, if possible, than that of the former place.

On entering the busy scene, the first object that strikes the visitor is the pale, business-like money-changer, his anxious forehead bedaubed with the white paint of his caste, peering over the pyramids of silver and copper heaped ostentatiously before him. Opposite, wrangling with half a dozen sepoys, in voices that might wake the dead, stands the noisy, energetic cloth-merchant, extolling his wares amidst the altercation with a fluency that would break the heart of a London Jew clothesman.

On each side, as you struggle onward, are squatted, in the peculiar Oriental fashion, venders of dried fruits, seeds, spices, opium, *cum plurimis aliis;* but your good-natured Arab charger halts in despair at the shop where yonder greasy cook is flourishing in his long, bony hands a wooden ladle, with which he bedaubs, in oily costume, a hissing mass of kabobs, or kidneys, which are emitting a savoury odour throughout that quarter of the bazaar, and engaging the attention of an impenetrable cloud of half-famished-looking wretches watching the inviting process. On extricating your embarrassed steed from this difficulty, and moving up another bazaar, at right angles to the former, the ears are saluted with the stunning and monotonous clang proceeding from the anvils of armorers and blacksmiths, who continue their noisy labour with an assiduity that, conjointly with their hissing fires and diabolical countenances, give an unpleasant presentiment of the world below.

Speckle the scene with a number of savage-looking fellows in dingy dresses, with matchlocks slung over their shoulders, a pair of business-like pistols, and a greasy-handled knife stuck in their belt, whilst a broad, iron-handled tolwar brings up the rear, and you will complete the best picture I can afford of Shikarpore bazaar, with its lazy, lounging soldiery.

CHAPTER V.

SIR JOHN KEANE'S force was advancing by another route, nearer the foot of the mountains of Beloochistan, towards the Bolan pass; and Sir Willoughby Cotton, thinking it prudent to secure that defile with the least possible delay, pushed on after one day's halt at Shikarpore. The commissariat subsequently urged this rapid advance as the cause of many difficulties, alleging that they had no time given them to make arrangements for the conveyance of supplies.

To enhance these difficulties, an order arrived from Sir John Keane, directing a large number of camels to be furnished by the Bengal commissariat for the supply of the Bombay troops, who were almost at a stand-still for want of carriage.* We had now scarcely a month's supplies for the army, and were about to enter a country of which little was known beyond native reports of its remarkable barrenness. Mehrab Khan of Kebat, the most influential chief of this portion of Beloochistan, had given the British agent assurances of furnishing the army with supplies, and, relying on his assistance, the forces advanced towards those sterile regions.

Mr. M'Naghten (the envoy to Cabul) received intelligence of the pass being occupied by the enemy, but he did not deem the source a creditable one; however, military precautions were properly taken, supposing the information correct.

The first march from Shikarpore was partly through a low jungle, which yielded, as we advanced, to a barren plain, that had lain apparently under water, and been recently dried by the powerful effects of the sun, which had cracked

---

* The cause of all this difficulty in procuring carriage for the Bombay army, was a demand of the Scindian camel-owners for payment from the time they were originally hired, which responsibility Sir J. Keane would not undertake, and the camel-owners refused to advance. The demand was no more than usual; and the results of this economy were injurious, and might have been fatal.

the surface with innumerable fissures. Not a shrub nor a blade of grass was visible, as far as the eye could reach, around this desert, which was bounded on our front by a lofty barrier of mountains, at about a hundred miles' distance. We had become nearly reconciled to barren views when they caused us no inconvenience beyond unsightliness; but when, after a wearisome night-march of twenty-eight miles over the desert, we reached our halting-place, where only two or three wells of muddy and brackish water (and these nearly exhausted) were found, matters began to look serious for man and quadrupeds.

Orders were sent to the rear to stop the progress of the army, whilst a wing of the 16th Lancers were detached, as a reconnoitring party, in advance. We started in the evening, and marched, till the following morning was well advanced, over precisely the same picturesque country, as far as the imperfect light showed us, for about thirty miles, when our eyes were rejoiced by the sight of a clear, rippling stream in the desert, near whose banks patches of grass and small fields of young wheat were growing, announcing the grateful intelligence of the desert being passed. Those who have suffered the pangs of thirst in a hot climate will estimate the feelings of the cavalcade as they hastened to avail themselves of the watery blessing.

Over the blighted waste we had crossed, (the Putt,) the deadly simoom occasionally blows in the hot season. Fortunately for us, we made the transit when the climate was moderate; but four months afterwards, two melancholy tragedies occurred to detachments marching to join the army in Afghanistan.

A portion of a native infantry regiment, escorting treasure from Shikarpore, were passing the desert in the night, when they mistook the way, and wandered the greater part of the next day in search of the track without meeting with any water to moisten their parched throats. One after another, they dropped, until two officers and twenty-one sepoys were lost. The remainder, many of them delirious, found the track and a stream of water in the evening.

The second catastrophe occurred to an officer of her Majesty's 17th Regiment, who with a serjeant and twelve men was sent to recover a gun which had stuck in the sand. The difficulty was greater than had been anticipated, and they were detained till mid-day, by which time the officer and eight men had fallen victims to the sun, and died raving mad. The serjeant and four men returned, debilitated for life, to report the success of the expedition.

The forces gradually closed to the front on receiving the report of the reconnoitring party.

Several marauding Beloochees, who had been hovering near us, committed a most impudent depredation here on some camels, which they carried off in broad daylight. General Thackwell, who was one of the sufferers, ordered a squadron in pursuit. Away we went, in full cry, at a hand-gallop, across some ten miles of country, mostly rocky, and intersected by numerous ravines; here and there, the steep and dangerous chasms were so artfully hid that it required a keen eye to avoid them. At length, we came to a halt, no Beloochees in sight, and our list of casualties great: three horses lame, and ten horses and men missing, who had been deposited in the cavities by the way. We now scoured the country in every direction, but found no suspicious characters, except in a small village, where the inhabitants forthwith protested vehemently that they were exceedingly honest people, which, of course, led us to suppose the contrary. It was now getting dark; and having no further evidence against the villagers beyond their own professions, we abandoned the pursuit, and reached camp soon after nightfall.

We resumed our march towards the mountains through a better country ; water was abundant, and occasionally a little grass was procurable for the horses, who were beginning to look much jaded.

On the morning of the 10th of March, we reached Dadur, which is close to the foot of a continuous chain of barren, rocky hills, and four miles from the gorge of the Bolan Pass. At this place, hopes were entertained that an abundance of supplies would be awaiting. Alas ! there were none—the commissariat were informed that the force had not been expected so soon, (a fortunate excuse,) and that consequently little was to be procured.

The melancholy truth transpired : there was absolutely not one day's provision for the army, and we were led to infer a similar fate at the places upon which we were about to march. The consequence was, an immediate reduction to half rations for man and beast; and Sir Willoughby saw that he had now no alternative but to push on through the mountain-pass, and take the chance of what might be found on the other side.

Major Cureton, of the 16th Lancers, who had been detached with a squadron of native cavalry, and a wing of a sepoy regiment of infantry, reported that no enemy was to be seen, but that forage was nearly equally scarce the first three marches in the Pass. The Bengal column being assembled at Dadur, orders were issued to advance, the cavalry-brigade being now preceded by the first brigade of infantry under Colonel Sale.

At daybreak, we reached the gorge of the Pass, which is wide enough to admit a regiment of cavalry in line. The road is level, but rocky; and through the centre runs a clear stream, with an abundance of long, coarse grass, nearly resembling dried flags, on its banks. The hills, without a sign of vegetation on them, rise abruptly on each side, at first, five or six hundred feet, but gradually increase in elevation as you advance. Our first day's march continued to follow the course of the mountain stream, on whose banks we encamped, surrounded by desolate and rocky hills. The camels had no food but the reedy grass, which contained little nutriment; but for our horses we had provided better, by carrying on from Dadur two days' supply of green forage. In the night, an alarm was given that the Beloochees had come down from the hills, and carried off some camels. As I happened to be on picket, a detail of my party went in pursuit, but no vestige of the robbers was found, and the clouds, which had long been lowering, now gave us such a sprinkling, that it was impossible to see twenty yards off, so the pursuit was abandoned.

In consequence of the tents being saturated with rain in the night, our march was deferred till mid-day, to give them a chance of being dried, for a wet tent and a bad road soon render camels unserviceable. We continued to march, henceforth, at mid-day, the weather being cool; and although a strong guard accompanied the baggage, the Beloochees managed to pounce upon some daily, plundering the camels and murdering our camp-followers. The infantry had frequent skirmishes with these marauders, but rarely succeeded in capturing any, so nimbly did the scoundrels mount the craggy sides of the mountains with their plunder and conceal themselves in ravines and caverns, which could only be approached at great disadvantage by the assailants.

The second march, we could scarcely move three abreast in many places, owing to the narrowness of the passage, (a chasm through a rocky mountain,) along which dashed a torrent, not deep, but extremely rapid. The sharp stones in its bed lacerated the horses' feet a good deal, and took rather severe effect on our bare-legged native followers. A man and horse belonging to the rear-guard of the 16th Lancers were lost on this march, but how the former lost his life is uncertain — he dropped behind his comrades on the line of march, and was never again seen alive.

Our three next marches were through a plain, environed by an amphitheatre of distant and lofty hills ; but the road was rough, nor was there any appearance of vegetation to cheer the miserable cattle. The camels dropped daily on the route in great numbers ; and many a tent, camel-trunk, and wine-chest, fell into the hands of our ruthless enemies the Beloochees, who doubtless celebrated several midnight orgies with our lamented luxuries.*

Three seers of grain (6 lbs.) per horse, and no grass, had reduced our steeds to mere apparitions, that stumbled mechanically onwards, having almost reached the valuable habit of living on nothing. The result was nearly the same as that

---

* It was afterwards known that these tribes had been in-stigated by Mehrab Khan of Kheiat to annoy us as much as possible during our progress.

which attended the horse of the Σχολαστικος, in the Greek fable, whose animal had learned to live upon nothing, but died shortly after trying the experiment.

Having ascended to a considerable height, the climate was fine, and we experienced no inconvenience from the sun ; but so dreary and oppressive to the spirits were these bleak and craggy mountains that frowned over us, and so jaded were man and beast, that it was with feelings of great relief in anticipation that we approached the termination of the dismal Bolan defile.

The most formidable position throughout the pass was certainly that which we reached just previously to quitting the above-named range of mountains. Having marched at midday, and ascended rapidly for about seven miles, we arrived at the passage I allude to, which was about twelve yards in width, over each side of which the high craggy hills beetled in irregular and threatening shapes. For a distance of about two miles we pursued the sinuous passage through this chasm,* looking upwards in amazement to find so formidable a succession of natural fortresses unoccupied, from whence a resolute body

* The rear columns were attacked here, but by a very small body of Beloochees, who soon retired.

of troops might have effectually checked our progress. A short distance beyond its gorge, we descended into an extensive plain, covered with a small aromatic plant resembling wild thyme, on which our cattle fed with avidity, and no wonder, for from recent appearances they must have conjectured that the earth had ceased to vegetate. Here, we expected to encamp; but water was found to be so scarce that the cavalry were ordered to proceed. We marched along the foot of a dark range of hills, from which the numerous lights glimmering through the darkness announced our old friends the Beloochees on the alert. About midnight, after a tedious march of thirty miles, we arrived at Sir-i-ab, which is called the outlet of the pass, although even here we lay in a valley flanked by lofty hills, whose summits were covered with snow. Of course, no tents or provisions arrived that night, but we were all too fatigued to grumble properly, and a cloak and saddle soon proved themselves effectually soothing.

After a halt of three days, the principal part of the force advanced to Quetta, a small fortified town, ten miles from Sir-i-ab, and about three from the hills on either side.

The plain was covered with the same scented plant we had seen before. Mint, tulips, hyacinths, and a great variety of wild flowers, enlivened the face of the soil.

Near the foot of the hills were several villages, mostly deserted, and groves of apple, pear, apricot, and plum trees, the luxuriant foliage and blossoms of which reminded us of the gardens of our beloved native country. The inhabitants of Quetta and its vicinity were rather shy at first, but finding we did not plunder them, they concluded we must be a set of fools, and resolved to profit by the opportunity.

Small quantities of grain, fruit, and lucerne were brought into our camp and sold at exorbitant prices; however, after the experiments which had been tried on our cattle and horses, we were only too happy to try and prolong their lives at any cost. Here the startling truth soon became known, that Mehrab Khan had formed no depôt of grain for the army. Sir Alexander Burnes, with Lieut. Pattinson and a few local horse, set out for Mehrab's residence, about eighty miles distant, in the hopes of inducing that treacherous chief to assist in procuring supplies; but this resource was now known to be almost desperate. In the meantime, foraging parties of cavalry ranged the country daily to procure fodder in the villages and amongst the fields.

Fortunately for us, a fine breed of sheep, known as the Dhoomba,* abounded here, and afforded no mean exchange for the tough and muscular flesh of such animals as had been brought from Bengal, and had walked into incredible condition, insomuch that they were now better calculated for supplying the artillery with traces than the soldiers with food.

Since entering Afghanistan, we remarked a material improvement in the dimensions and looks of the inhabitants, compared to the natives of the other side of the Bolan mountains. Their dress was mostly composed of sheepskins, camels'-hair, and other warm materials, requisite from the coldness of the climate, even at this season: the thermometer stood about freezing-point at daybreak; but Quetta is table land, nearly six thousand feet above the sea.

Women, except the old or very young, were nowhere to be seen, so prevalent were their unjust suspicions of our behaviour.

Our diet was now one that should have gladdened the heart of the doctors, (of course I speak only of military ones,) being confined to bread, mutton, and water; for those who had been fortu-

* The Dhoomba sheep is so named from Dhoom, the tail, which grows to a great size with this species.

nate enough to get wines and other luxuries as far as the Bolan pass, had almost all been obliged to drop them ere they quitted that gloomy defile, to carry absolute requisites, such as a tent and clothes; and fortunate were they who even accomplished that object throughout the campaign.

As there were few regiments able to keep up a mess, an application was made by the officers to be allowed to draw the same rations as were issued to the soldiers. This was refused; but subsequently we were allowed to draw on the commissariat for one bottle each week of a fiery, unwholesome spirit, made in India, and called arrack.

The audacious attacks made upon our people and cattle by the Kaukers, a tribe of hill-bandits, made it hazardous for any one to stray beyond the outposts. Every night some unfortunate camp followers, returning from seeking grass or tending cattle, were murdered, and usually mutilated in a wanton and barbarous manner.

Before leaving Quetta, an opportunity occurred for a small retaliation on the savages.

An alarm having been given early in the day that a party of Kaukers were hovering near the outposts, Lieut. Yule, of the 16th Lancers, who was on picket with a party of his regiment, turned out in pursuit. Within two miles of camp, he perceived a party of about thirty Kaukers, armed with swords and matchlocks, retiring towards the hills on foot; when pursued at speed, they fired and wounded one of the Lancers, and separating, some escaped to the hills, whilst others threw themselves into a small mud fort, whence they fired on the cavalry party, but without effect. Yule, having dismounted his men, scaled the fort, killed seven inside, and took one prisoner, mortally wounded, whom Sir J. Keane (who had just arrived in camp, and assumed command of the army) immediately ordered to be hanged. The next evening ten more who had been taken prisoners were also hanged on trees near Quetta.

Notwithstanding this salutary example, a daring attack was made immediately afterwards on our cattle, by two or three hundred of the same tribe. At mid-day they issued from the mountains, cut down several surwans,* and carried off a number of camels; but a wing of an infantry regiment and a squadron of cavalry coming up, the marauders retired, driving their booty to the hills, which were so precipitous, that many of the camels were recovered, being abandoned by the Kaukers in their retreat amongst their native crags.

* Surwans are camel-drivers.

Sir Alexander Burnes having reached Mehrab Khan's residence, now sent intimation that no assistance could be expected from that chief, who, so far from procuring grain for the army, had instigated the tribes to annoy us in every way, and to conceal or carry away the produce of the country. Time could not now be wasted in punishing Mehrab for his duplicity, but a day of severe retribution awaited him on the return of the Bombay division of the army from Caubul.

Our position was now far from comfortable. If the army advanced, and all supplies were removed out of our way by the natives, starvation and the loss of all our cattle appeared the probable result. And in case of a retreat through the Bolan pass, every crag would, of course, have held an enemy to oppose such invaders. Independently of this, the moral effect of a retreat at the commencement of a campaign would have been in the last degree disastrous; yet such an alternative was advocated by many officers on whose shoulders the main responsibility did not rest. Sir John Keane could not but see that entering the Bolan pass was the passage of the Rubicon, and orders were issued for the army to advance towards Kandahar on the morning of the 7th of April: the men were reduced to an allowance of one pound of flour, and non-combatants to half a pound per diem; meat and spirits were issued as usual.

No grain was in store for the cavalry, but the horse artillery were allotted rations of three seers a horse daily, without which the guns could never have been drawn. The cavalry troop horses subsisted almost entirely on green wheat, collected by foraging parties. The officers were occasionally able to purchase small quantities of barley, or Indian corn, for their chargers, by paying an exorbitant sum to an Afghan extortioner.

On the morning we left Quetta, fifty horses of the cavalry brigade were shot, in the lines, being too weak to carry their load. This melancholy process of slaughtering horses was repeated daily, before or on the march.

The first morning, on leaving Quetta, we descended, through a steep and rocky pass, into an extensive valley. A few scattered villages were seen, whose inhabitants had betaken themselves to the hills, whence they sallied occasionally to commit atrocities on any stragglers from the lines in retaliation for the damages committed by the camp followers on their habitations, and by our horses on their corn fields.

It was carefully circulated amongst the natives who came near us, that grain and all other supplies would be paid for, and also that a reimbursement would be made for damages done to their property. It was further hinted to them that we were friends (not enemies) who were bringing a virtuous monarch to rule their country; but this they were unable to comprehend.

As we advanced, however, the same system prevailed with the inhabitants, and not a soul was to be seen in the villages or on the line of march, except when levelling a matchlock from some almost inaccessible crag. Our foraging parties occasionally found young wheat fields, which were demolished in a few minutes; but had it not been for that inestimable little aromatic shrub, which grew in the most hopeless solitudes, it would have been impossible for us to proceed, as it afforded almost the only food for the camels and beasts of burden, as well as fuel for the army, which it would have been a difficulty to dispense with, man having been essentially a cooking animal from the days of Prometheus, before whose well authenticated exploits it is difficult to say how mortals fared.

Having crossed a succession of rocky mountains and barren valleys, the fourth march from Quetta brought us to the Pisheen valley, which is said to be the best cultivated part of lower Afghanistan, which it might well be without exhibiting much fertility.

The valley is very extensive, and appeared, as we advanced into it, to be well inhabited. The corn and barley fields were rich and numerous. The natives of Pisheen had not deserted their homes, and flocked to our camp, bringing camels, horses, bullocks, sheep, and grain for sale, but all at the same exorbitant rate which had been exacted at Quetta. The better class of inhabitants, terming themselves Synds, or descendants of the Prophet, (the prolific Mahomet,) were well attired, and certainly the finest men I have seen in the East. I was much taken with a richly-mounted cimeter worn by a noble looking Afghan, and endeavoured to tempt his cupidity by offering in exchange a pair of English pistols liberally bedizened with silver ornaments, money being out of the question, as that article was more than usually scarce, and more than usually necessary, in those days of famine : but though the pistols took his fancy much, they still did not succeed, and he returned them, saying, "It would be unjust to take these weapons which you will soon stand in need of, for the Ameers of Kandahar will meet you in the field before you have approached much nearer their city." "We shall be happy to see them," I replied, " and after the rencontre, cimeters will be cheap and plentiful in the British camp."

The Synd had some authority for his assertion, as that day intelligence was received that the Kandahar chiefs were concerting measures to oppose our advance.

Kandahar was under the control of three princes, Kohun Dil, Raheem Dil, and Mehn Dil, Khans, brothers of Dost Mahomed, but never on amicable terms with the Caubul monarch.

The authority of the Kandahar chiefs had been long unpopular; but of late their oppressive rule had rendered them more odious, as the exactions on the inhabitants had been increased in order to levy an army to oppose the British invasion.

The northern side of the Pisheen valley is crossed by a range of mountains called the Kojuck, a rugged pass leading to Kandahar. Brigadier Arnold rode forward in the evening to reconnoitre this defile, and, on reaching its gorge, found the heights occupied by a party of horsemen, who fired upon him; but a small party of sappers ascended and dislodged them. A spy was also observed lurking near camp at night, and was shot by a sentry of the 13th Light Infantry.

The 1st brigade of infantry led the way through the Kojuck pass, and were followed next morning by the Cavalry Brigade, who started two hours before daybreak. On entering the pass, about five miles from camp, we found it completely blocked by the camels of the preceding brigade. Having halted for about three hours, until these obstacles were removed, we commenced the ascent — the dragoons dismounting and leading their horses, whilst a party was detached from each squadron to assist in dragging the guns of the Horse Artillery.

The dry bed of a torrent, winding round the foot of a precipitous mountain, was the course by which we commenced the ascent. Having followed this track a few hundred yards, we struck off on a road which our sappers had cut on the side of the mountain, and up which the guns were drawn with considerable labour. We were occupied a great part of the day in surmounting this steep and rough ascent, casting into the ravine beneath the dead bodies of men, camels, and bullocks, who had been murdered the night before by our restless old friends the Kaukers.

By four o'clock in the afternoon, the cavalry and artillery reached the summit of the pass. From this elevated position we looked down on a barren, extensive plain, on the edge of which the snowy tents of the 1st brigade formed the only interesting object, as they intimated a termination of our labours for the day. A fine mountain breeze was whistling over the heights and overcame the sun's influence.

We were astonished that the Kandahar chiefs had not occupied this defile, which had taken us much labour to surmount even with the indispensable aid of the sappers, and unmolested by the enemy.

With the aid of our glasses, we discerned a few spies or marauders (probably both) among the rocky peaks, watching our proceedings, but keeping out of musket-shot from the native infantry pickets, which crowned the neighbouring heights.

Our descent of the Kojuck was even more precipitous than the ascent, and many a horse and camel ended his weary career on this precipice during the night.

When we bivouacked at sunset, the agreeable intelligence was made known of no water having yet been discovered, and of course no food was procurable, the commissariat stores being far behind. The soldiers stood the want of food for twenty-four hours of hard labour without a murmur; but when they heard no water was procurable, they gave vent to many a hearty malediction on these inhospitable regions. Several started off to the hills with waterskins on their backs, and returned after a long search, the greater part unsuccessful, but some few with a little filthy mud and water, which was swallowed with an avidity that extreme thirst only could produce.

As very few tents had made their appearance, and the night was wearing apace, we laid ourselves on the least rocky piece of ground that we could select in the dark, and rested till three in the morning, when the musical invitation of the trumpet called us again to the saddle, and, after a march of eighteen miles across the desert plain, and under a sun which, in these lower regions, did not spare us, we came at length to a small pond of dirty water, where we halted.

I threw myself down beside this inestimable puddle completely exhausted ; and my horse having taken a drink, which threatened rivalry with Munchausen's notorious steed, followed my example ; but our repose was soon cruelly interrupted by a requisition for our services on outlying picket, some two miles in advance. We both arose, stretching and shaking ourselves into consciousness ; my charger certainly yawned widest, although I explained to him how much he had the best of it, as no dread of a court-martial need await him for sleeping on his post.

My tents and servants did not arrive till late next evening, having been absent three days without leave, and leaving me to luxuriate during that time in the same clothing, and on a loaf of tolerably hard and stale ammunition bread, about the *weight*, size, and *consistency*, of a twelve-pound shot.

We had been compelled to halt here, to enable the rear-guard to come up, who had been frequently fired on by the Kaukers; but no casualties occurred, which does not say much for our enemies as marksmen, though the long rifle, termed a "jezzail," which they use with a forked rest, carries a great distance, and with tolerable accuracy, when properly handled.

Some camels and servants belonging to the rear-brigades were shot in the transit of the Ko-juck Pass, and many of the officers' and soldiers' tents and baggage were plundered; but these unaccountable mountain warriors almost invariably allowed the cavalry to pass unscathed through defiles, where they would have been almost helpless if attacked.

Amongst other troubles and privations, we had

now daily to reckon the badness and scarcity of water. The wells being dug in ground whose surface was white with saltpetre,* we found the water partook so strongly of this mineral, that it was not only nauseous to the taste, but affected man and beast with a diarrhœa, which, combined with the fatigues and exposure to which all had been subjected, reduced the greater part to a debilitated condition.

As we had descended a good deal since leaving Quetta, the heat of the sun daily increased; and although we marched every morning long before daybreak, the roads were so bad and our cattle so weak from want of sustenance, that we had generally to pass the noon-day unsheltered.

On the 23rd of April, we had, according to the most prevalent conjectures, arrived within about fifty miles of Kandahar, and met no enemy. Having marched about twelve miles in the morning, we reached our appointed ground for halting about nine A.M., when some assistants, in the quartermaster-general's department, reported to the brigadier of the cavalry that the water in camp†

---

* The cold of Afghanistan may be partly owing to the great quantity of saltpetre diffused over its surface.

† On a more accurate survey of the country, water enough was found here to have sufficed the whole army.

would barely suffice for a brigade of infantry. We were accordingly ordered to remount, and proceed towards a river, which was supposed to be some ten miles' distant. Few who were present will ever forget that dreadful march. The reflection of the sun from the burning dust and barren hills was so dazzling, that many who underwent it have never recovered their strength of sight. We had marched about ten miles, when the halt was sounded. It was mid-day; about twenty men of the leading regiment held together, the remainder of the cavalry-brigade were straggling over four or five miles of country in the rear; some were urging their jaded beasts with the spur, some leading them on foot, and others driving their chargers before them at the point of the lance or sword. But far the hottest thing I beheld that day, was the talented Colonel Ninny, purple with heat and anger, and seeking an object to vent it upon.

"Where the devil is your squadron, sir?" was demanded, in a voice of thunder, of a ponderous captain, with a face like a salamander, and a corporation like a hogshead.

"Four miles behind, sir, at least," replied the hogshead, proud of having got so far along the road, (as well he might be.)

"How dare you, sir, give me such an answer, and leave your squadron behind?" cried the enraged genius.

Poor hogshead, frothing with excitement, turned round in search of relief, and lighting on the officer in charge of his troop, poured forth the full tide of his indignation on him for not bringing the stragglers to the front.

"And pray, sir, where is my troop?"

"Here are the serjeant-major and two privates; the remainder vary from four to five miles in the rear; and as I could not carry them, they are left behind," replied the troop-leader.

"There is no excuse," cried Ninny.

"But, sir——"

"Hold your tongue, and join your troop."

This was conclusive, and broke up the agreeable interview.

When the sun had begun to decline upon the scene of suffering he had caused that day, the river was descried from the brow of a sandy knoll, winding its shining path through the sterile soil. Man and beast rushed in uncontrollable confusion to the waters, and quenched the fiery thirst under which both had suffered severely.

Our baggage did not arrive in camp till about midnight; and so severe had been the heat, that almost every dog belonging to the officers of the brigade either dropped dead on the road, or was long in recovering the effects of the cruel experiment. Many men were much broken down, and one or two in the hospital doolies died on the road.

The cavalry-brigade alone having advanced, and intimation having been received that the Kandahar chiefs, with three or four thousand cavalry, had left the city to attack us, General Thackwell considered it probable that they would attempt a surprise that night, as their spies would probably have time to inform them of our forced march. Accordingly, pickets, consisting of about one half of our force, were posted to protect the remainder, and sentries, videttes, and patrols, with loaded pistols and carbines, spent the evening of that merciless day in watching for any approaching party. Our vigilance was all in vain: the Kandahar chiefs did not deserve the compliment we paid them; and we lay on watch all night, undisturbed by any sound more warlike than the complaint of a camel, or the bray of a donkey.

The next day, I was sent with a party of four men to reconnoitre some hills about three miles distant, on the opposite bank of the river, and finding many deep ravines in the way, I left my party behind, and fording the stream, ascended the heights, where the sand was so deep, that my charger sank up to his knees at every step. I was about half way up the hill, when an Afghan, armed to the teeth with tolwar, matchlock, and pistols, started suddenly from a cavern behind a rock, a few paces above me. I drew a pistol from my holsters, and levelling it at him, recommended him to surrender. He stood a few seconds, apparently irresolute; then darted behind the rock, which was close beside, and out of my sight. I spurred forwards through the sand to meet my friend on the opposite side; but he had ascended by a narrow ravine, and in a few seconds I caught sight of him among some crags, about fifty yards above me, and in full retreat.

I pursued again, but in vain; for the mountain, which had now become rocky, presented obstacles every ten yards; and when I reached the summit, I caught a glimpse of three or four mountaineers a few hundred yards from me, stealing round the mountain, apparently with the intention of intercepting my retreat. No signs of a camp or any body of men were to be seen in the plain, as far as my glass enabled me to discern; I therefore descended the mountain on the opposite side from which I had ascended, perceiving that my *longue* carabine attendants were prepared for a shot, which I preferred making a difficult one.

Having reached the foot of the mountain, I stirred my Arab's mettle across the plain, receiving three or four salutes from my polite acquaintances above, some of which whistled as if they had been well directed.

Having struggled through a quicksand, which lay between me and the bank, I recrossed the river, and joined my party on the other side.

I have little doubt that the men I encountered on the hills were spies from the Kandahar army. The matchlock of the Afghan I came upon unawares, must have been unloaded, or he would certainly have tried to prevent my ever reporting our interview. I might easily have sent a pistol-ball through him, for he was not ten paces from me; but it looked so much like murder that I could not draw the trigger.

Marching from hence by the banks of the river, we reached an inhabited village, in which a little grain was procured for our famished horses. News arrived in the course of the day that the Kandahar chiefs had given up all thoughts of opposing us, and retreated towards Herat, leaving the field open to Shah Soojah. That illustrious monarch preceded us next day to Kandahar, where, from the confused salute we heard in the evening of cannon, matchlocks, and various noisy instruments, we conjectured he had been received with tumultuous joy. Public exultation is a cheap commodity at all times, but never less valuable than when inspired by personal fear; and the citizens of Kandahar were actuated, I think, by interested motives towards their new monarch. History assigns no cause he had ever given to render himself popular.

The defection of Hadji Khan (chief of the Kaukers) was the cause assigned by the Afghans for the Kandahar chieftains abandoning their territories without a struggle; but as they could not, at that time, muster above five or six thousand troops, it is probably as well for them that they did not make the experiment.

Some days before we arrived, they advanced a few marches, with the intention of attempting to surprise us by a night attack; but afterwards hearing that we were not all in the habit of going to sleep at night, they retired to Kandahar, to deliberate on the subject, and thereby saved the army of the Indus from utter and immediate destruction.

Hadji Khan, who had been long in correspondence with Burnes, and also in the confidence of
the Kandahar Ameers, was not a bad specimen of
a traitor. His whole life had been devoted to the
profession, and he had risen by it from an obscure
station to considerable influence, changing his
politics with the times, and also his friends, when
more influential ones presented themselves. Believed and trusted by all, he was faithful to none.

This clever traitor now attached himself to
Shah Soojah, being the first chief of any influence
who joined that monarch.

CHAPTER VI.

KANDAHAR—MURDER OF LIEUT. INVERARITY—THE ARMY CONCENTRATED—ADVANCE BY THE VALLEY OF THE TURNUK UPON GHUZNI.

On the morning of the 27th of April we entered the plain in which Kandahar is situated, and encamped about two miles from the city. This plain is well irrigated and tilled. Gardens enclosed by high mud walls, and abounding with a great variety of fruit, are seen on almost every side on approaching the city; and so level is the plain in its vicinity, that nothing could be discerned but a long mud wall with a few domes looking over it. The wall which encloses Kandahar in an oblong figure, (whose perimeter exceeds three miles,) is flanked by numerous circular bastions, and defended by an irregular dry ditch. The curtain is about twenty feet in thickness at the base, and its relief varies from thirty-five to forty feet, according to the depth or shallowness of the ditch. In the parapet are numerous embrasures and loopholes for matchlocks or jingals. I need scarcely annex to this brief description that it is a place of no strength.

The bazaar runs from the Shikarpore gate, by which we entered, across the city, and is intersected at right angles by a similar bazaar from east to west. At the point of intersection is a large dome, which affords a respite from the sun, now becoming intolerably hot. The city was thronged with inhabitants, in every variety of Eastern costume, busily engaged in their various avocations; and notwithstanding their material change of administration which took place yesterday, business seemed to be going on as quietly as if nothing unusual had occurred. From the estimate formed on that occasion, I should say the natives of Kandahar were not very violent politicians.

The women were clad cap-à-pie in a flowing white robe, (not always particularly clean,) in which a piece of netting was inserted over the eyes, to give them an opportunity of seeing what was passing; although it precluded them from what is said, perhaps unjustly, to constitute a source of satisfaction amongst northerly dames— being seen. A neat green or scarlet leather slipper gave some relief to the ghostlike appearance, and generally attracted observation to a pretty foot.

The palace is situated in the southern quarter, and surrounded by a high shot-proof wall, which was garnished by several old guns of curious workmanship : a legend is attached to some of them, which is not likely to be interesting to the world at large.

An abundance of supplies were procured for the army in Kandahar, and the surviving horses of the cavalry brigade (nearly three hundred had died on the march) once more tasted grain : but the relief came too late with many, whose hearts had been broken, and the greater portion never recovered condition.

About a fortnight after our arrival, the Bombay division joined us, consisting of a wing of H. M. 4th Light Dragoons, H.M.'s 2nd and 17th Regiments, two troops of Horse Artillery, 1st Native Cavalry, 19th Native Infantry, and two companies of Foot Artillery ; and now, for the first time, the " Army of the Indus" were assembled, though many hundred miles distant from the river in whose name they were baptized.

The Bombay force had suffered less from famine than ourselves, having marched a shorter distance, and been better supplied with grain: two thousand camel loads were dispatched for their use from Shikarpore, to the grief of the Bengal commissariat.

In May, the hot winds set in with much virulence, and the heat in our tents became very oppressive. In spite of every effort on our parts to reduce the temperature by throwing horse-cloths over the canvas, and keeping wet grass, day and night, against the doors, the thermometer stood at 110° during the heat of the day, and did not fall more than twelve degrees at night. The camp, which was now a long standing one, became exceedingly offensive, owing to the number of dead cattle in the vicinity, principally camels; and the swarms of flies that worried us, enabled one to comprehend what that visitation must have amounted to when sent to plague the Egyptians.

The hospital began to fill rapidly. By the middle of May ours held more than one fourth of the regiment to which I belonged. Jaundice, dysentery, and fever were the prevalent complaints;

the two latter, far the most fatal. The 13th Light Infantry and Company's European regiment were very severe sufferers, and were ultimately reduced from sickness and death to a very weak state, especially the former, who buried more than an average of a man a day during the two months we halted at Kandahar. The causes of these complaints, independent of heat, were the bad water drank on the march, and the dampness of the soil in the neighbourhood of the city.

The people of the country being apparently better disposed towards us now than at first, the officers of the army strayed occasionally some miles from camp on fishing and shooting excursions, until these amusements were checked by a tragical event, which occurred on the evening of the 28th of May.

Two officers of the 16th Lancers, Lieuts. Wilmer and Inverarity, were returning towards camp on a sporting excursion rather later in the evening than usual. On ascending an eminence, about four miles from camp, (having given their guns to the grooms to carry,) Inverarity preceded his friend, and rode to the top of a rocky hillock, from whence the camp fires were visible. When he reached this spot about twenty Afghan savages rushed upon their unarmed victim, tore him from his horse (as supposed), and inflicted several mortal wounds with their cimiters. Wilmer, following, unconscious of what had occurred, was suddenly attacked by some of the same gang. Providentially he had a thick walking stick in his hand, which he raised in time to parry the first blow made at his head, and, escaping from his assailants, descended the hill, pursued by the assassins. These he soon distanced, and reaching an outpost of irregular horse about a mile from the place, returned with some of the party in search of the banditti. The cowardly villains had absconded, leaving poor Inverarity covered with wounds, but still alive. He spoke but a few words, faintly describing how he had met with the disaster, and begged for some water, which, as soon as it could be procured, he drank, and almost immediately afterwards expired.

In the dead of night the party arrived in camp with his corpse, so gashed and disfigured, that it could scarcely be recognised by his brother-officers, and the following day his remains were interred with the usual military honours in front of the standard guard.

The malice of his murderers rested not even in the grave, for some months after we heard of a gang (who came from the direction of the place where he was murdered) attempting to dig up his body. Having demolished the tomb, they were interrupted in their accursed project by a party of native infantry quartered in Kandahar, and fled to the hills.

Inverarity's remains were afterwards removed from the spot, and interred in the city of Kandahar.

The barbarians who, it is supposed, committed the deed, were subsequently secured by the exertions of Major Mac Laren* of the 16th Native Infantry, while storming a small fort near Khelat-i- Ghilzie. Some articles, supposed to have belonged to Inverarity, were found in their possession; but the punctilious judge did not consider them legally identified, and the assassins were liberated, about in sufficient time, it was conjectured, to fall in with another officer, who was murdered between Kandahar and Caubul.

Had the detection and punishment of the murderers been committed to Shah Soojah (as he requested) there is every reason to suppose they would not have escaped so easily, and the business would have afforded his Majesty sincere pleasure.

Rumours of Dost Mahomed's preparations for an obstinate resistance were now reaching us

---

* This gallant soldier fell at the battle of Sobraon.

daily; but the envoy frequently expressed his firm conviction that no opposition would be made. Sir John Keane differed in opinion, and refused to leave the Bombay division behind, according to Mr. Mac Naghten's suggestion, unless the envoy could guarantee that Dost Mahomed would surrender.

This was of course out of the question, and it was at length determined that the whole force should advance, except a small garrison for the city. The commissariat exerted themselves to complete their arrangements for the march, and the approaching departure was joyfully welcomed by the army.

A Kafila, with grain from Shikarpore, arrived opportunely in camp previous to our move, under the escort of two regiments and some local horse, despatched from Kandahar to protect this caravan, as news had been received that two chiefs of the powerful Ghilzie tribe were preparing to pounce on the convoy.

It was fortunate that this precaution had been taken; for it was ascertained that a large body of the enemy had made preparations to surprise these necessary supplies on the road, and the fidelity of the merchant who brought up the caravan was somewhat doubted, until the arrival of the reinforcement put treachery out of his power.

In the beginning of June, the force under Brigadier Sale, which had been detached soon after our arrival in pursuit of the Kandahar chiefs, returned. Those princes had fled to Girishk, a fortress about eighty miles distant from Kandahar, and near the Helmund river, but abandoned it on the approach of their pursuers, and fled towards Herat.

Thus ended, in the most undignified manner, the authority of the three Ameers, for the present. It is singular that in such extremities the scheme of a reconciliation with their brother, Dost Mahomed, had not been resorted to, for it would have been unquestionable policy in that monarch to insure the re-establishment of the Kandahar chiefs to them in their principality, in case of the united forces succeeding to repel the British invasion.

It is evident, however, that no such measures could have been preconcerted to oppose our advance, from the non-occupation of the Kojuck and Bolan passes. The Afghans, near Kandahar, informed us that the chiefs distrusted their subjects, and perhaps with cause.

Weak both in mind and authority, these chiefs

hovered irresolutely around their capital, but abandoned the power they had usurped when danger accompanied its retention.

On the 27th of June, our camp was struck, and the Cavalry division, with the 1st Brigade of Infantry and head quarters, preceded.

Next day, came the second Brigade, Shah Soojah and his motley procession, which swelled daily in numbers, with hordes of Afghans, who came to join the Shah and tender their allegiance (as they affirmed), but in reality, no doubt, to watch the progress of events: to remain *faithful* in case of success, or plunder in case of a reverse.

The Bombay division of Infantry, under Brigadier Willshire, brought up the rear. One regiment of Bengal Native Infantry and the heavy guns were left at Kandahar.

Most of our officers were on the sick list, and on the remainder the duty was severe, consisting principally of guards to protect the baggage, and pickets. The outlying cavalry picket was ordered, by the commander-in-chief, to take post four miles in advance, where, of course, no baggage was allowed, nor even a groom (strictly speaking) to hold your charger. This picket was posted at nightfall, with orders to fall back on the main picket, in case of feeling an enemy. The main picket was usually posted about a mile from camp, consisting of a squadron of cavalry, four companies of infantry, and two six-pounders, from whence a chain of pickets communicated along the front and round the flanks of the army, whence patrols from the rear-guards completed the circuit.

The third day's march brought us to the Turnuk river, which is a clear and shallow mountain stream, running through a valley sown abundantly with barley and Indian corn. The water was excellent, and supplies for our cattle were daily procurable; but numbers continued to die, unable to overcome the debility ensuing from previous overwork and starvation.

The natives of the valley were peaceable agriculturists, who came constantly into our camp, bringing for sale corn, eggs, fowls, and fruit; but the mountains which flanked our march, at a short distance, were amply stocked with marauders. The sickness under which the army had long suffered now began to abate, or at least, to assume a less virulent character; but the appearance of the sufferers was materially altered. Those of previously stout and portly figures were seen walking about in clothes once fitting closely, but now hanging down like empty pudding-bags; and faces, whose rubicundity once emulated the richest hues of Chateau Margaux, now wore a puckered-up, gamboge aspect, which made sympathy no easy matter with those who were prone to laughter.

Many who had never much flesh to spare, were reduced to varieties of angular shapes, which might have been useful to a mathematician when studiously inclined, on the line of march. Such had been the devastating effects of dysentery and fever on most of the community.

The zealous and able managers of the intelligence department had prophesied that we should probably be seriously molested by the tenants of a strong fort in the Ghilzie country, seven marches from Kandahar, called Khelat-i-Ghilzie.

A bribe had been sent to the two principal chiefs of the Ghilzies,* accompanied by a letter from Shah Soojah, desiring their assistance. The money was retained, and an insulting answer of defiance returned.

On approaching Khelat-i-Ghilzie, the adjutant-general of cavalry was sent, with a small escort, to reconnoitre the place.

* In the subjugation of this country in 1840, this tribe of Ghilzies were found the most obstinate and inveterate foes to British influence. Khelat-i-Ghilzie was gallantly held by a native infantry regiment (which now bears the name) against frequent attacks of the Ghilzies during the insurrection.

The brigadier commanding the advanced guard of two squadrons of cavalry, two guns, and a small body of infantry, on approaching this memorable place, espied two or three hundred well-armed Ghilzies on an eminence not far from the road.

Having minutely examined their position, the brigadier pronounced it to be remarkably strong, and prudently resolved to await the arrival of the main body of the army, previously to dislodging the party.

Whilst revolving in his mind the most advisable method of attack, unfortunately, the head of the column hove in sight, and the doubtless brilliant result that might have ensued was precluded by the Ghilzies taking to flight.

It was considered fortunate that the enemy knew not their own strength, or that a more rash officer had not been in command on the occasion, who, in attempting to intercept the retreat of the Ghilzies, might have incurred serious responsibility.

Sir John Keane, on his arrival at the encamping ground, was so satisfied with the arrangements, that he is reported even to have instituted a comparison between the gallant colonel and the Duke of Wellington, in his usual energetic and classical mode of expression.

As we had ascended considerably since leaving

Kandahar, and were frequently on high table-land, the heat ceased to annoy us so severely as during the three preceding months, and we considered we had overcome by far our most formidable enemy in the relentless sun.

Various and contradictory rumours continued to pour daily into camp. At one time, it was said that Dost Mahomed, at the head of an army of thirty thousand men, with eighty guns, had taken up a strong position near Caubul; at another, that his chiefs and Kuzzilbaches (Persian mercenaries) having deserted him, he had despaired of making any effectual resistance, and fled towards the Hindoo Koosh. Lastly, we were informed that he had detached two of his sons, with chosen men from the army, to garrison the fortress of Ghuzni; but the same evening, perhaps, merchants would travel through our camp, *en route* for Kandahar, and declare they had left Ghuzni but a few days, and had not seen a single soldier in the place! These reports, when compared with the actual events, are more reconcilable than appears at a first glance.

Small parties continued to arrive daily, and tender their allegiance to Shah Soojah; and we were authentically informed, that the two before-mentioned Ghilzie chiefs, with about five or six thousand horse each, were moving daily on both flanks, parallel with our line of march, and would neglect no opportunity to harass the army. Of the truth of the latter part of the information, we entertained no doubt, *provided* they could do it with impunity.

About seventy miles from Ghuzni, we quitted the rich valley of the Turnuk river, and crossed an extensive, well-cultivated plain, thickly studded with small mud forts. The inhabitants of this part of the country dare not dwell in open towns or villages, owing to the numerous bands of marauders infesting the neighbouring mountains, who have no mercy on the defenceless villages.

Small, but luxuriant groves of fruit-trees, bending beneath their loads of rosy-cheeked apples, speckled the plain, and formed a pleasing resting-place for the eye, fatigued with the ceaseless range of barren mountains skirting the valley.

On the 20th of July, we reached a small place called Nance, about twelve miles from Ghuzni; and as yet no authentic intelligence had been received of Dost Mahomed's intentions or movements, nor of any steps having been taken to interrupt our progress.

Sir John Keane, however, received news at this place which induced him to order the rear column to close up to us in the evening. The fort was said to be garrisoned by a body of Dost Mahomed's troops; and Ufzul Khan, his second son, was supposed to be near us with four thousand cavalry. As it was probable that Ufzul Khan would effect a junction with the Ghilzie chiefs, and attempt to surprise our camp during the night, the whole army were drawn up in line on their standard guards soon after sunset, and lay under arms during the night.

Nevertheless, nothing certain was known regarding these reports. Major Garden, the quartermaster-general, had ridden to reconnoitre Ghuzni in the evening, and perceived no signs of its being garrisoned.

At daybreak, on the morning of the 21st, our line broke into three columns, the cavalry on the right, the artillery in the centre, and the infantry on the left, and in this order advanced over the plain, at the extremity of which the fortress of Ghuzni is situated.

As we approached, a nephew of Dost Mahomed came to tender his submission to the Shah, and gave information of the fort being occupied by Hyder Khan, a son of Dost Mahomed, with a garrison of three thousand infantry and a few cavalry; but he expressed a suspicion that they would evacuate the place. This individual complained of having been ill-treated by his uncle; but there appeared little doubt that the gentleman came into camp merely as a spy.

Reports from the advanced parties continued to state that no garrison was to be seen on the ramparts : however, we continued to advance in the same order.

When within about a mile of the walls, a smart fire of matchlocks was suddenly opened on the advanced guard of infantry on our left, from a small village, and from behind some garden walls. The column immediately halted ; the 16th Native Infantry were detached to clear the village, in rear of which was a small redoubt, protected by the fire of a bastion of the fort, on which the Afghans fell back.

Two officers,* and several men of the 16th Native Infantry, were wounded by the Afghans in the skirmish.

The artillery now swept past us, and took up their position on an elevated post in a village about four hundred yards distant from the nearest bastion of the fort. At the same time the 4th

* Captain Graves and Lieutenant M'Mullen, 16th Native Infantry.

Dragoons were ordered to the rear to protect the baggage, which, it was supposed, was likely to be attacked by a body of the enemy's cavalry, which had been descried on the right, moving in that direction.

The remainder of the cavalry-division were drawn up in close column of squadrons, about three quarters of a mile from Ghuzni, and supplied escorts to the reconnoitring parties.

The garrison now opened their fire upon us, which was answered by our artillery from the village, but the guns, which were only six-pounders, were found to have little or no effect on the walls, in consequence of which they were soon withdrawn, having lost two or three horses from the enemy's fire. Sir John Keane, in his despatch, assigns as a reason for this eccentric cannonade, a desire to unmask the enemy's batteries.

About the same time the infantry were also withdrawn, and bivouacked in rear of some gardens, enclosed by mud walls, and about a mile from the fort.

The cavalry entirely escaped his excellency's notice. Early in the day, several troops had been detached with the different reconnoitring officers; but now being of no further use for the present, we were left standing to our horses' heads, and meditating on what kind of service we could be employed while the rest of the army were bivouacked.

At length, the garrison, being unemployed for the present, pitied our forlorn condition, and prepared to provide for our amusement. A monstrous gun from the citadel, carrying a sixty-eight pound shot, was seen to be trained with much assiduity, in our direction, and we awaited in agreeable suspense the result of the process.

Two little tents had been procured by some of the officers, and pitched on the spot where we had dismounted. Some luxurious fellows had been out on a foraging excursion amongst the baggage, and returned laden with a supply of bread, fowl, cold meat, and milk. This collation was being discussed, and a vote of thanks to the industrious foraging party was in the act of passing, when a loud report from the citadel interrupted them, followed by a load of iron hurtling over our heads, and plunging amongst the mass of baggage and camp followers in rear. This was immediately succeeded by another, better directed, which cut the ropes of our neighbours' tent, wounded one of their servants, and killed a trooper of Native Cavalry.

I never saw two tents struck with such admirable alacrity as on this occasion. I am sure I do not exaggerate when I say that in less than two minutes the tents had disappeared, and the spyglasses of the inmates were directed at the walls to ascertain the cause of this uncourteous interruption.

The senior officer present now ordered the cavalry to mount, and we retreated half a mile to the rear, through the midst of a mass of baggage which our camp followers were hurrying off with incredible despatch, perceiving the probability of their becoming a target for the merciless Golundauze in the fort.

Scarcely had we picketed our horses, when the trumpet called us again to the saddle, and we changed position to the northern front of Ghuzni, on the Caubul road, and about a mile from the nearest bastion. We reached this ground about sunset; but the infantry, who passed by a more circuitous route, round the other side of the fortress, did not arrive in camp many of them till near midnight.

An incessant fire of cannon, matchlocks, and jingals, was kept up during the night on the troops whilst marching, and after their arrival in camp; but the enemy lost a night's rest, and wasted their ammunition to very small purpose.

As they had done us very little injury in the daytime, the night fire was not a subject of much apprehension; but all Asiatics have much confidence in great noise and constant firing, without taking pains about its direction and effect; it keeps up their courage by diverting their thoughts.

At daylight the following morning, from the intelligence received, and the observations of reconnoitring parties, we were better enabled to judge of the difficulties opposed.

Ghuzni is situated in a plain, which it commands easily on every side but the north, where a small range of hills run down to within one hundred and fifty yards of the walls. It is built on a low extensive mound, the foot of which is surrounded by a mud rampart, flanked by numerous circular bastions. The curtain of this enceinte varied from thirty-five to forty-five feet in height, and averaged perhaps twenty in thickness, which rendered it shot-proof to our artillery, as our heaviest guns had been left at Candahar to be sent as a present to Prince Kamran of Herat!

The rampart was defended by a deep wet ditch, over which permanent bridges were built at the gates.

The citadel stands on a rock on the central

and most elevated part of the mound, commanding the whole of the town, and about two hundred and fifty yards of the hills on the north, and is surrounded by a thick mud rampart, defended by a fausse-braye. The soles of the embrasures and loop-holes in the parapet of the latter were not sufficiently depressed to enfilade the approaches to the citadel.

The gates were all blocked with masonry excepting that which leads to Caubul, and this was built of massive wood, strengthened by iron clamps and bars, and defended by the cross fire of two adjacent bastions.

Hyder Khan, a son of Dost Mahomed, commanded the garrison, which consisted of three thousand infantry and one thousand four hundred cavalry: amongst the former were about one hundred artillery-men, who had deserted or been reduced in the East India Company's artillery.

The heights on one side of the plain were occupied by a body of about three thousand cavalry, commanded by Ufzul Khan; and on the other, a body of infidels, of similar strength, but infantry, were posted to harass our left.

It was also conjectured that the two Ghilzie chiefs who had been hovering on our flanks on the line of march, had joined their forces with those of Ufzul Khan; and these chiefs were reported to be in command of eight or ten thousand horsemen.

The news of Runjeet Singh's death (which occurred on the 27th of June, 1839) having set Dost Mahomed's mind at rest, regarding any serious co-operation on the part of the Sikhs against him, he was now preparing to move down with all the forces he could assemble, and attack us whilst engaged with the siege of Ghuzni.

His eldest son, Mahomed Akbar Khan, had been detached with about five thousand men to the entrance of the Khyber pass, which Colonel Wade was preparing to enter, in company with the Shah Zada Timoor, Shah Soojah's son.

Colonel Wade commanded a few companies of native infantry and some raw levies, and was supported by a Sikh auxiliary brigade.

Before Colonel Wade entered the Khyber Pass, the Afghan force under Mahomed Akbar had been recalled by Dost Mahomed, under the urgent circumstances then pressing upon him; and the Khyber was entrusted to the defence of the wandering tribes of Khyberees who infest those extensive ranges of mountains.

Our own *effective* force now scarcely amounted

to two thousand eight hundred European cavalry, infantry, and artillery, and about four thousand sepoys: so much had the army been reduced by sickness, death, and the detachments left to garrison the places we had passed through—viz., Bukkur, Shikarpore, Quetta, and Candahar.

Exclusive of these, of course, were the Shah's troops, whose contingent, in case of an action, would, it was conjectured, be fully employed in watching the numerous Afghan rabble which flocked around Shah Soojah. These had now swelled to a large amount by the daily influx of armed horsemen, who were as likely to be spies and adherents of Dost Mahomed, as friends of Shah Soojah.

At the best, the bare suspicion of treachery from this armed host rendered it necessary to keep a force on the watch, and the contingent must have been used for that purpose in case of a general engagement.

On the morning of the 22nd of July, Sir John Keane and the engineers were actively employed in reconnoitring the fortress.

Captain Thompson, the chief engineer, having completed his observations, and remarked that a communication was kept up by the garrison with the exterior, through the Caubul gateway, gave it as his opinion that apparently the most practicable means of assault were presented by a coup-de-main, in lieu of a regular assault, (for which we were not provided,) and suggested as a method to attain this purpose, that the Caubul gate should be destroyed by bags of powder.

Some officers were in favour of an immediate escalade, but as that method would necessarily involve a greater loss, and might still remain in reserve, in case of the failure of the former and more expeditious method, Sir John Keane resolved on adopting Captain Thompson's suggestion.

During the morning of the 22nd, we were most of us endeavouring to make amends for the two days and nights of almost unremitting vigilance that had been exercised, when the shrill tones of the alarm trumpet rang confusedly from many quarters of the camp, and caused us all to start up and prepare for the saddle. A smart rattling fire of musketry, interrupted by the occasional roar of cannon, was heard, apparently near the foot of the hills, on our left flank, and a hurried report ran along the lines, that Dost Mahomed, with his whole army, had come suddenly upon us.

We were now become too well used to our

harness to take long in preparing, and a very few minutes served to show us formed, on our alarm posts.

The Bengal cavalry brigade were immediately dispatched at a round pace towards the scene of action. The ground we passed over was rough and undulating, and in many places covered with crops of high standing corn, which completely intercepted our view; but the nearer rattle of musketry indicated we were not far from the field of strife.

Having ridden over about two miles of country, of the above description, we came upon an open and barren plain, which extended to the foot of the hills, where we descried some of Shah Soojah's contingent, accompanied by two or three guns, closely engaged with a body of two or three thousand Afghans.

On our approach, the Afghans commenced a retreat upon the hills, pressed hard by the Shah's troops, who were unable, however, to bring their guns far up the hill-side.

The cavalry brigade were detached by wings of regiments to the flanks and rear of the heights, in order to intercept the enemy, should the infantry succeed in dislodging them.

The Afghans having ascended to the summit

of the hill, took up a hasty order for battle, and awaited their enemies. A deep ravine skirted the base of their position, and its crest was occupied by a party of matchlock-men, thus enfilading the approach by the only practicable ascent. The Shah's troops were not inclined to storm this strong defensible position, but halted behind the ravine, and under cover of rocks and broken ground endeavoured to drive the enemy from the heights by musketry; but the distance between the skirmishing parties, to admit of either fire being very galling, was much too considerable.

We remained watching the skirmish taking place on the heights, in expectation of seeing a reinforcement arrive from camp, which would enable the infantry to dislodge their enemies, and force them into collision with us; but the commander-in-chief refused the application for reinforcements, being resolved to keep the infantry fresh for the work which awaited them on the morrow, and Shah Soojah would not part with any more of his guards. A body of cavalry, as a last resource, endeavoured to mount the hill side, and take the Afghans in reverse, but after ascending a few hundred yards, the rocks and ravines became so numerous that the ascent was quite impracticable, and they reluctantly descended under a harmless salute from the enemy on the summit.

At sunset, the forces were withdrawn to camp, having killed about sixty Afghans, and taken fifty prisoners, with a loss of only a few wounded on the side of the British.

The prisoners being brought into the presence of Shah Soojah, declared they were Ghazees, or Crusaders, bound by a religious vow to take his head, and that the oath of the party would sooner or later be accomplished, although they had not been successful in the present attempt.

" I will, at all events, secure your head now," replied the indignant monarch; and beckoning to his executioner, (who was never far from his master's side, knowing the Shah's predilection for the office,) the speaker's head rapidly disappeared.

The comrades of the decapitated being loth to part with this useful article, showed signs of resistance, when the brave and zealous attendants of his majesty rushed upon the unarmed prisoners, unrestrained by word or gesture of their king, and massacred their victims.

One old man, it is said, escaped to tell his comrades in the mountains the fate of the captives.

And this act was perpetrated in the midst of the first Christian army which had set foot in Afghanistan since the creation of the world.

Let it not be supposed that the suppression of the murder lay in the power of the British authorities; there was not, I believe, one British officer present, and the whole merit rests with Shah Soojah; but he was viewed as a mere puppet in our hands, and on us, throughout Asia, will rest the obloquy of this savage massacre. No doubt the Afghans have done as bloody deeds, but it became, therefore, more incumbent to show a better example.

CHAPTER VII.

STORM AND CAPTURE OF GHUZNI—ADVANCE TO MEET DOST
MAHOMED—HIS ARMY DESERT HIM, AND HE FLIES TO-
WARDS THE HINDOO KOOSH.

THE plan of operations against Ghuzni having
now been arranged, general orders directed the
troops to move as quietly as possible from their
quarters to the allotted positions. About three in
the morning the artillery had occupied the heights
near the Caubul gate of the fort, and about three
hundred yards from the ramparts. The infantry
were drawn up in columns of companies on the
road beneath the hills, and to the left rear of the
artillery. The cavalry were posted round the
fort to intercept the retreat of the garrison and
the advance of relief.

The 16th Lancers were on the Caubul road, in
the rear of the infantry, as a diversion was ex-

pected from the enemy's cavalry in the mountains, in favour of the besieged.

The morning was exceedingly dark, and all around quiet as death; for the garrison, who had hitherto kept up an almost incessant cannonade, seemed to think they had done enough, and were enjoying repose. We began to imagine that they had used up their ammunition in the past vigorous efforts to alarm us, and that the fort had been evacuated.

This oppressive silence was interrupted by the word of command passing down the ranks in a whisper; and the forlorn hope moved to their post near the Caubul gate, to await the result of the engineers' experiment. The bags of powder, amounting to three hundred pounds in weight, were carried by the sappers, supported by a party of European volunteers; and the engineer officers, who placed the powder at the gate, distinctly heard the voices of the Afghan-guard conversing near the gateway. The saucisson was laid, and fired by an officer of the Bengal Engineers.

Suddenly, a broad glare lit up the ramparts, and with a smothered, crushing report, the Caubul gate was shattered into innumerable fragments. In one moment, the face of nature seemed to have awoke in uproar. The rushing and confusion in the city, and on the ramparts, was accompanied by a hasty and random fire from any gun which could be manned, no matter where it was pointed. The whole city, aroused instantaneously from repose, and yet too late, hurried in confused masses to man the walls, ignorant of the disaster which had befallen the gateway. Then burst from the hills the solemn, majestic roar of our artillery; light flashed upon light in uninterrupted succession, and the shell, sped on its mission of death, curved steadily through the lurid atmosphere.

The fort continued a random answer from its guns, and hung out lights from the walls, to discover the locality of their assailants; but this served to direct the fire of our artillery, and the walls were soon cleared of their occupants. The wing of a Native Infantry regiment, posted on the south-eastern front, drew a part of the besieged in that direction, to repel this false attack.

Under cover of the artillery fire, sweeping the parapets, Colonel Dennie, leading four light companies from the 2nd, 13th, 17th, and Company's European Regiment, advanced to storm the Caubul gate, closely followed by Brigadier Sale, in command of the main body of the storming party, consisting of the remainder of those four British regiments.

The enemy opened a smart fire of matchlocks upon the advance, and the gateway was found much obstructed with rubbish and splintered, beams from the demolished framework. The postern, turning sharply to the right, and leading to the interior of the place, induced an officer in the passage to suppose it blocked up, in consequence of which, he took upon himself to order a bugler to sound the retreat; but the advanced party having penetrated to the interior, heard, or heeded not, the recal.

Overcoming every obstacle, the gallant Britons rushed, with a loud cheer, through the postern, at whose entrance they were met by a body of Afghan desperadoes, who had thrown themselves devotedly into this passage, resolved to defend it with their lives. Here, the struggle was short, but deadly. Armed with sword and daggers, each Afghan fought and fell, with his face to the enemy; and if a spark of life remained after he had been hurled to the earth, his last act was to direct a sword or pistol against the breast of his hated foe as our men trampled over him in their ownward career. So confined had been the area for combat, that many of the soldiers, being unable to use their weapons at full length in the mêlée, unfixed their bayonets, and used them as daggers;

and the broken and blood-stained weapons told with what effect they had been wielded.

The resistance at the entrance having been overcome by the destruction of this desperate band, the cry was, "On—on ! to the citadel !"

A panic had now seized and paralysed many of the garrison, for they huddled together in confined spaces, and stood to be slaughtered like sheep, or rushed in frenzy to the walls, and cast themselves from the parapets.

No thought of refuge and opposition in the citadel seemed to have occurred to any, nor had it been sufficiently equipped for defence.

The efforts of the most rational were directed towards an escape outside the walls, by secret outlets; but there, the clear light of morning, and the sabres of the cavalry, left slender hopes of escape.

As daylight brought each minute tracing of the works into view, the gallant British regiment were seen winding up the steep, rocky ascent which led to the citadel, where, with a wild " hurrah !" they burst the gate, mounted the ramparts, and cast loose the gay blazonry of their banners to the wind as it moaned along the shattered battlements of captured Ghuzni.

Scattered parties of the besieged now fled to

the tops of the houses, whence, after they had recovered a little from the prevalent panic, a desultory fire was maintained on our soldiery. This useless resistance nullified all attempts to restrain the carnage which ensued, and which the garrison, by not surrendering at once, brought upon themselves. So determined were many to carry war " to the knife," that they would discharge their last pistol at the party advancing to capture them, and then resign themselves, sullenly, to the fate which followed this last act of outrage in the shape of a bullet or a bayonet. Probably, they imagined that no quarter would be granted them; " the quality of mercy" being rarely found " dropping like the gentle dew from heaven" on the rugged surface of Afghanistan.

Possibly, the intelligence of yesterday's massacre of the prisoners by Shah Soojah might have induced them to expect a similar fate in captivity.

A brigade of sepoys which had entered the town and spread on the ramparts, having scoured the buildings, soon cleared them of their defenders, and put an end to all resistance in a few hours, the British regiments being withdrawn to their lines.

Confusion, however, continued to prevail

throughout the day, for a herd of about one thousand two hundred horses belonging to the garrison were dashing wildly through the town, driven frantic by wounds or alarm. An officer, with a party of dragoons, was sent into the fort to secure these horses, which now resembled wild beasts more than domestic animals; and it was with much difficulty this roving band were at length secured and led off. Very few horses of much value or of sufficient size and strength for a cavalry remount were selected from these captives. Those, however, which were used for that purpose have mostly proved active and hardy animals, and are considered by many superior to the general run of stud-bred horses in Bengal.

In the course of the day, Hyder Khan, the governor of Ghuzni, was captured, and brought into camp, where Shah Soojah, at the instigation of the commander-in-chief, reluctantly granted him his life, which the Shah no doubt considered forfeited, for bearing arms against a king who had been deposed before, or very shortly after, the delinquent's birth.

Not so fared Woolee Mahomed, (a relative of Dost Mahomed, and standard-bearer of the army,) who defended himself to the last extremity in the cellar, where he had taken refuge, close to his Zenana,* which he protested should be entered by none, save over his dead body. He surrendered, ultimately, to two officers on political employ, who ventured to promise that his life should be spared, and was brought before the tyrant Soojah, who immediately ordered him to be executed.

It has been alleged that Woolee Mahomed had proved treacherous to the Shah in some previous intercourse; but no sophistry can prove that Shah Soojah was then a king, when Dost Mahomed sat on the throne, and, with the approbation of his subjects, exercised supreme authority.

Many causes, too numerous to dwell upon, have been assigned for this act of severity, by those desirous to defend Shah Soojah, but none apparently can justify so cold-blooded a murder, when the words of two British officers had been pledged for the safety of the unhappy victim. Surely, blood enough had been shed that day to appease the royal resentment, had it been confined to anything resembling moderate limits.

Amongst the besieged the carnage was found to be considerable. Upwards of seven hundred bodies were interred in the fort, and about two

* The Zenana is the sanctum allotted to the ladies.

thousand were taken prisoners. It was impossible
to ascertain the number of wounded, for many
crawled out of their hiding-places, in the city,
several days afterwards, and were taken charge
of by such of the citizens as had resumed their
usual avocations; and in the villages, some distance from Ghuzni, a few days afterwards, I found
several, dreadfully scorched and wounded, who
admitted they had escaped over the walls, on
the morning of the storm, shortly before daylight.

Nearly all the prisoners were liberated, by
direction of the commander-in-chief, in the course
of the day; for this, there was no alternative, as we
had not the means of taking charge of and support-
ing such a large body of men, in the present state of
affairs, and this act of clemency, it was supposed,
would produce a beneficial effect in the beginning
of the campaign.

Amongst our own troops, the list of killed and
wounded amounted to two hundred, but of this
number not more than thirty were killed, or died
of their wounds. In the list of wounded were
nineteen officers, but none of their injuries proved
fatal. Some had been wounded by a short barbed
arrow or bolt, shot from a cross-bow, which imple-
ment the Afghans are tolerably expert in using;

but these weapons had been in the hands of the townspeople during the defence. The garrison had been selected from the best of Dost Mahomed's troops, and were about three thousand in number, and universally well equipped and armed.

Among the prisoners were found several Golundauze or Foot Artillery, from Hindustan. One of these declared that, the day preceding the storm, he had suggested to the governor the probability of our attempting to blow in the gate of the fortress, and recommended that a palisade should be thrown across the entrance; but his advice had been disregarded, the gate being considered strong enough to resist any attack.

The place being now in our hands, guards were posted at the gate, and parties patrolled the town to prevent any more plundering, and to collect the prize property.

Eight pieces of cannon, of various calibres, and twenty two jingals, or wall pieces, were taken. Among the ordnance, was our old antagonist of the 21st instant, which was found to carry a sixty-eight pound shot, though assuredly at greater risk to the artillerymen who were rash enough to fire it than to the enemy, for the interior was curiously honeycombed.

Few things of much value were taken except

horses, of which about one thousand were picketed in front of the 1st Cavalry Brigade, but owing to the insufficiency of ropes and picketing pegs, the greater part of the horses broke loose during the night, and more than half escaped or were stolen!

The whole of the prize property taken at Ghuzni, when sold, it is said, fetched less than three lakhs of rupees, although the horses, arms, and other articles, when put up for auction, sold for most exorbitant prices, and the amount was realized in a few weeks. Yet an impenetrable veil of mystery encompasses the subject. No officers to the present date have received any part of the treasure; and information, though frequently and publicly solicited, has been equally scarce.

After the capture of the fort, the enemy, who had occupied the adjacent heights, retired, and left us for awhile at rest. Parties of Afghan horsemen arrived daily in camp, from Caubul and its vicinity, to tender their allegiance to Shah Soojah. These people concurred in asserting that Dost Mahomed was still at Caubul, collecting his forces to give us battle, and that his present army amounted to fifteen thousand men and forty guns.

On July 27th, a deputation under Jubbar Khan

(brother of Dost Mahomed) arrived at our out-posts, and were conducted to head-quarters. They came to inquire what terms would be granted to Dost Mahomed by the British government.

They were answered that Dost Mahomed must surrender himself into our hands, and return with a portion of the army to Hindostan, where a jageer would be allotted him, and a pension of a lakh of rupees annually.

Indignant at the severity of the terms, the Af-ghan ambassador replied nearly as follows:—

"These proposals are so insulting that I will not even mention them to my brother; for what less could have been offered had you already vanquished him in the field? We have hitherto heard that the English were a just and equitable nation; but on what plea can you found the right of dethroning a monarch, the choice of his country, and placing on the throne yonder deposed puppet whom I spit at?* You have taken our stronghold of Ghuzni; you may also, perhaps, overcome the army which my brother has raised to defend himself; but the eyes of all Asia are upon you. Asiatics will judge and appreciate your conduct; and the blood of those innocent men who fall in

* This compliment was addressed to Shah Soojah.

the contest rests on your own heads. May Allah
defend the right !"

I have rarely heard a speech more to the purpose,
and never one more difficult to answer.

Jubbar Khan, having made more than half his
auditors look uncomfortable, returned to Caubul,
after resting a short time at the quarters of his
friend, Sir Alexander Burnes, who spoke of him
in the highest terms. Jubbar Khan had formerly
been ill treated by Dost Mahomed, and been
estranged thereby from his brother ; but now that
adversity loured, forgetting all former differences,
he came to tender what service lay in his power,
and remained faithful to the last, although through
his friend Sir Alexander Burnes, he might, doubtless, have provided well for his own interests. A
rare example of disinterestedness, and almost a
solitary case, according to all accounts of Afghan
character.

Jubbar Khan's escort consisted of about one
hundred cavalry, who were nearly all uncommonly
fine and powerful-looking fellows, mostly clad in
chain armour, and armed with lances and matchlocks, but mounted on horses apparently not up
to their weight : these animals, however, are more
active and hardy than would be supposed, and
are trained to perform long journeys at a shuffling

I 2

pace of about five miles an hour, and frequently on very short allowances of fodder.

On the morning of the capture of Ghuzni, the Cavalry Brigade turned out about eleven o'clock, in consequence of the approach of a large body of horsemen, which proved to be Hadji Khan, Kauker, with his followers. He had kept some distance in our rear since quitting Kandahar, and now pushed forward to join us, seeing our affairs wore a more favourable aspect. This chief had maintained a correspondence with the political agent since the army had entered Afghanistan, offering to remain with the Kandahar chiefs, and do them all the injury in his power until our arrival! Yet Hadji Khan never actively assisted the army, nor did he restrain his people from committing depredations whilst we were passing through his own hills. He now came forward with a camel load of letters, (an excellent pretext,) asserting that he had been earnestly engaged in collecting and forwarding our communication. His influence might possibly have effected that object, without remaining two or three marches in rear with his whole force. This new addition augmented the Shah's force to so large a body of Afghans, that they were prudently kept at arm's length; for treachery from that camp was now quite as formidable as resistance from the enemy in our front.

On the 30th of July, we advanced from Ghuzni towards the capital, the cavalry brigade preceding as before, accompanied by the first brigade of infantry. Colonel Roberts's brigade followed, next day, with the Shah; and General Willshire's division formed the rear-guard of the army.

At the commencement of the march, we passed through a narrow defile, which would have been an admirable position for Dost Mahomed to hold during the siege of Ghuzni, or to select afterwards to oppose our progress. The summit of this defile was found to be the highest ground we had crossed, being fully 1000 feet above the site of Ghuzni, and that fortress was computed at nearly 8000 feet above the level of the sea.

Having traversed a considerable tract of rocky undulating ground, we entered, on the third day's march, a small but well irrigated valley, where the turf and bright corn fields beneath us, partially shaded by avenues of fruit trees, nourished by the friendly assistance of a mountain stream, whose course they closely and eagerly pursued to the end of the valley, presented a prospect which would anywhere have been admired, but, in these barren regions, it looked like

> " That vale enchanting
> Where all looks flowery, wild and sweet,
> And nought but love is wanting."

Possibly, on reflection, we might have found other wants; but at present it was necessary to dispense with wishes and encounter stern reality.

Several deseterrs of Dost Mahomed's army joined us here, with intelligence of his being in position about thirty miles from us, at a place called Urghundee, with a force of fifteen thousand men and thirty pieces of cannon; but the deserters suggested that he would probably advance to meet us at Maidan, an open ground, which sloped gradually towards a rivulet lying in our route. On receipt of this news, orders were issued to the rear columns to close immediately to the front, and we marched next morning about ten miles in momentary expectation of encountering some of the enemies' advanced posts. Our pickets were strengthened and carefully disposed along the front; and our men, elated at the prospect of the approaching struggle, burnished their arms and looked keenly to the condition of their chargers and accoutrements. Every heart beat high in the confident anticipation of shortly essaying what might be effected by a small band of resolute and disciplined soldiers against this overwhelming mass of vaunting Afghans, who amounted to more than double our numbers.

Such were the hopes entertained by our army; but, ere mid-day, these brilliant anticipations were given to the winds; for a large body of Afghans arrived at our pickets, bringing accounts that Dost Mahomed's army was breaking up and deserting; and that, in despair, he had abandoned them and his guns at Urghundee, and fled towards Bameean. This news was soon after confirmed by numerous bodies of the ex-king's cavalry arriving in camp to tender their useful submission and services to Shah Soojah, until in the hour of need they might find it more profitable and less dangerous to choose another master.

Major Cureton, with a squadron of the 16th Lancers, one of Native Cavalry, and a few artillerymen, was immediately despatched to take possession of the cannon. Twenty-five pieces were found in position under the brow of a hill, near Urghundee, about twenty-two miles distant from our present encampment.

At the same time, Captain Outram, A. D. C.* to the commander-in-chief, with twelve other officers, and about two hundred and fifty Native Cavalry, undertook the pursuit of Dost Mahomed towards the Hindoo Koosh. Hadji Khan, Kaukur, volunteered to act as their guide, and to assist in capturing the late monarch with several hundred of his Afghan retinue; but these rapidly decreased in numbers as they approached Bameean.

The gallant Outram, whose whole life has been a scene of daring exploits, which obtained for him the appropriate designation of Bayard, " Le chevalier sans peur et sans reproche," has sketched, in his "Rough Notes," the details of this expedition, and I shall therefore not presume to trace that ground.

Thus was the object of this singular campaign accomplished, and Shah Soojah, after an exile of thirty years, re-established in his dominions. The feeble resistance offered by Dost Mahomed was a matter of surprise to all the army, considering the character for enterprise, courage, and ability universally assigned him, and which the earlier period of his career fully testified; but he had been many years a king, which may perhaps

* Governor of Scinde, afterwards, or as it was then designated, "Political Agent."

account for the difficulty. Possessing such strong natural obstacles to the advance as well as maintenance of an invading army, as Afghanistan uuquestionably does, he profited by none of them. In the most rugged and formidable defiles, a few marauders only were posted to assail our rear guards and baggage ; and even these not always at the suggestion of their prince, but to glut their own appetites for blood and plunder. As we advanced through the inhospitable regions of Lower Afghanistan, the inhabitants generally fled from before us, but often left their standing crops for the maintenance of our cattle. Had these been cut down and carried away to the mountains by the villagers, our horses must all have died, for they endured, even as it happened, starvation enough to destroy half and enfeeble the remainder.

Though many opportunities presented themselves for cutting off our supplies of water, this expedient was only once or twice attempted, and that in so slovenly a manner that a party of twenty or thirty troopers sufficed to restore the water to its channel, unopposed by the enemy. These circumstances amply prove, without entering further into details, that Dost Mahomed had neglected the important opportunities which lay in his grasp, of multiplying our difficulties at the outset. He might assuredly have induced the chiefs of Kandahar (his own brothers) to make common cause against their common invaders, and, in conjunction with the Ghilzie chiefs and Mehrab Khan of Khelat (both of whom, as well as their adherents, showed abundant proofs of their readiness to bear arms against us) dispute the passage of the numerous and difficult passes we were compelled to traverse. This supposition may be fully warranted by the reply which Burnes describes Dost Mahomed to have given on a former occasion to the Kandahar chiefs, when threatened by the Persians. "When the Persians approach, let me know; and as I am *now* your enemy will I then be your friend."*

Such would have appeared the most rational course to pursue; and had he taken these measures and executed them with vigour, there is little doubt that his own army would have remained faithful to him when the prospect appeared favourable, and when an example should be set by other tribes. It is no matter of surprise that an army of lawless tribes should desert a chief whom they deem unable or unwilling to direct their efforts to the best advantage.

* Vide Burnes' Travels, vol. iii. p. 272.

The chieftains, whose aggregate force would have been considerable, were allowed to be beaten in detail, or to abandon their position as we advanced. Mehrab Khan, with two thousand brave followers, fell in the defence of his fortress, even after the dethronement of his sovereign. The Kandahar chiefs, with what remained of their army, having lingered to the last moment, were compelled to abandon their city without a struggle. The Ghilzie chiefs were willing enough,* as they afterwards proved, to meet their invaders in the field, and their numbers must have been considerable, as more than six thousand were known to be moving on our flanks on the advance to Ghuzni.

Lastly, a garrison of less than three thousand men in a fortress, which, by the modern rules of the art of war, must inevitably fall in a few days, (considering the Gothic tracing of its defences,) was the forlorn bulwark opposed by the monarch himself to the approaches of his capital.

However, this dernier resort, even, was made the least of by his majesty's unaccountable desire to linger near the capital. Had the defile, five miles on the Caubul side of Ghuzni, been selected as a

* The Ghilzies were the chief actors in the insurrection and massacre of 1842.

position for his army, they would have been advantageously placed to intercept our advance upon Caubul, and from thence dispositions might have been made for the relief of Ghuzni, or to surprise us by a chupao, or night attack, which mode of warfare has often been successfully practised among the Afghans. What might have been the result of such a manœuvre it is difficult even to conjecture ;* for in the darkness of night many advantages of discipline are lost, where the enemy is felt before he is seen, and fire is almost as likely to tell upon friend as foe ; their habit, it is said, is to attack the rear of camp, where the confused mass of cattle driven from the bazaar into the lines must create no trifling confusion amongst the troops turning out to form on their alarm posts.

The fall of Ghuzni greatly dispirited Dost Mahomed's army ; † they became distrustful of him, and he of them, and the result was a mutual separation.

Many of his soldiers concurred in stating, that

* One of our chiefs suggested, in the event of a night attack, that the men should remain in their tents, and fire upon the assailants from the cover thus afforded.

† They expected Ghuzni to detain us many months, judging from the difficulties it had presented in recent periods of Afghan history.

they had assured Dost Mahomed of their faith, and would have abided by him; but when it became known that Jubbar Khan had proceeded to Ghuzni to open a negotiation, they doubted him, and concluded he was about to provide for himself at their expense.

Taking all these circumstances into consideration, this campaign, in an abstract military point of view, has thus far turned out more fortunately, and with less and feebler opposition from the enemy, than the most sanguine of its instigators or conductors could reasonably have anticipated.

Politically, I shall not discuss the subject, because I could never perceive one sound reason for taking the haphazard and unprofitable tour.

On advancing towards the position lately occupied by Dost Mahomed, nearly the whole line of march was flanked by troops of the deposed monarch. Many of them were well mounted, and all well armed, although little uniformity was maintained in dress or weapons.

Some wore steel caps and gauntlets, chain-armour variously wrought, and light, neatly-finished cimeters, which bore a remarkably keen edge, owing to the hardness of the material; others were clad in padded cotton or silk dresses, of every variety of colour, the head being covered by turbans of thick and embroidered Cashmere, or plain white muslin. They carried over their shoulders long matchlocks, inlaid with silver or ivory.

The Kuzzilbashes, or Persian mercenaries, were the only troops amongst whom prevailed any uniformity, and they were generally distinguished by a high, black, sheepskin cap, with a small red cloth top, and a sort of frock dress, generally white, which reached to the knees, opening in four places from the waist. Light deerskin boots, fitting closely to the leg, completed this plain and serviceable costume.

Amongst the cavalry were certainly some of the handsomest and most powerful-looking fellows I ever saw; the complexions of many were fairer than those of some of our own sunburnt veterans; and amongst them, also, were some of the dirtiest, long-bearded, ferocious-looking savages I had hitherto seen: men who would doubtless have taken no small pleasure in carving and dissecting any luckless straggler from our camp whom they might happen to meet singly and unarmed. The descriptions I have read of the Huns and Goths who overran the Roman empire in the fifth century, forcibly occurred to me as I marked their personification on each side of the road, unaltered and unimproved by a lapse of fourteen centuries; while the western emigrants have progressed to a state of civilization and intelligence, having subverted nations and monarchies in their resistless course.

As we surmounted the hill near Urghundee, which is flanked by dark lofty mountains, without a trace of vegetation, the peaks of the Hindoo Koosh were visible, glittering in the morning sun from their snowy summits. The intervening country, to the foot of this mighty barrier of Afghanistan, presented a most unattractive appearance : an undulating, rocky soil, with a few patches of short dry grass, extended apparently a great portion of the way towards their foot.

The guns remained in the same position in which they had been left by Dost Mahomed, on high ground, and were ranged to command a gorge from which our army issued. The ground, in front and rear, was flat and favourable for cavalry, in which his principal strength consisted. All that was requisite for the fray was a little more heart and less distrust.

CHAPTER VIII.

ARRIVAL AT CAUBUL—DEATH OF COLONEL ARNOLD—RETURN
OF THE EXPEDITION IN PURSUIT OF DOST MAHOMED—
THE RUSSIAN BUGBEAR—FALL OF KHELAT.

On the morning of the 6th of August, the army
moved through a well-irrigated and woody valley,
to the foot of a small hill, on the further side of
which lay the celebrated metropolis of Afghanistan.

Next morning, accompanied by some of my
brother officers, I visited the city of Caubul,
which lies under some steep and rugged hills at
the extremity of a flat and extensive valley, whose
site at the city was estimated at six thousand five
hundred feet above the sea. On surmounting the
eminence on its western side, Caubul appears to

great advantage, lying immediately beneath, with the white tops of its various structures peering out from amongst thick groves of almond, walnut, plum, and various kinds of fruit trees which flourish in this quarter of the city. Crossing a bridge over the Caubul river, and winding through some narrow lanes, on each side of which were houses surrounded by gardens, we entered the principal bazaar, which extends completely across the city to the gates of the Bala Hissar, or Shah's palace. At the commencement of the bazaar, we were much struck with the appearance of the fruiterers' shops, where grapes, peaches, melons, pomegranates, and other fruits, were tastefully hung amidst branches of trees, to which they were suspended. This street entered a small square, which looked much like an European market-place, the centre being occupied by stalls of vendors of vegetables, milk, and ice, while the houses in the square were occupied by tea, spice, and sherbet merchants. The sight of the latter soon brought our party to a halt to enjoy the unwonted treat of a bowl of iced sherbet. In Kandahar, the sherbet was also sold cooled with snow, but the ice was acknowledged to be a great improvement. From the further side of this market-place, an arched bazaar, occupied entirely by silk and cloth merchants, conducted us into a second square, tenanted by shawl makers and dyers. Thence we passed through another well-thronged arcade into the third square, where resided the tanners and dressers of sheepskins, for which Caubul is celebrated. These skins are very neatly dressed, the wool being worn next the body, and the exterior tastefully ornamented by embroidery in silk of different colours. During the cold season, the working classes usually wear long jackets of these skins, with short sleeves reaching to the elbow, whilst the merchants, and those unaccustomed to manual labour, adopt a warmer but less commodious mantle, which reaches to the ankles. The black lamb-skins, brought from Bokhara and Persia for the manufacture of caps, are highly prized; they are made of the skin of the lamb immediately after its birth, and are extremely soft and glossy.

Beyond this square, the bazaar becomes more narrow, and much more noisy, as you enter the quarter occupied by saddlers and armorers, who form no inconsiderable portion in the manufacture of articles so requisite and so much used in this land of violence. The saddlery is made of durable materials, though clumsily put together; and in the armorer's shop,* it is a rare thing to find a piece of good steel among the many fantastically shaped weapons, where the ingenuity of the workman appears to have been called in play to invent these fanciful methods of inflicting torture on his fellow-creatures.

The Bala Hissar, standing apart on a mound which overlooks the city, is surrounded by a rampart garnished with circular bastions, and parapets, similarly to most of the fortresses of the East. The wall was in somewhat bad repair on our arrival, but this was soon remedied after the Shah had taken up his residence there. The place is of no importance as a fortress, being completely commanded by the range of hills in its immediate vicinity. The palace itself conveyed little idea of grandeur to the spectator; but Shah Soojah took pains in rendering it more consistent in appearance with the notions he entertains of the dignity and state requisite for the abode of so mighty and independent a monarch.†

* The best cimiters are of steel made in Persia, where they are so hard and highly polished as to take the keenest edge; but this makes them necessarily very brittle.

† Had the Shah paid less attention to *meretricious* ornament, and more to its defensive requisites, it would have contributed much to his credit and safety.

In a burying ground, near the Bala Hissar, was found a tomb, with an English inscription, to the memory of one John Hicks, who died A.D. 1666. This monument formed a plentiful subject for conjecture as to who this individual could have been, who had penetrated into a country infested from time immemorial by hordes of robbers, who consider all travellers, especially when alone and unprotected, as their legitimate property. The Afghan tradition was, that two Europeans had arrived with a Persian caravan in Caubul, and had entered the service of the Shah of Afghanistan, and that this monument had been carved and built by the survivor.* But what brought these adventurers into Afghanistan is likely to remain a matter of some ambiguity at this distance of time, especially as the *biographer* of John Hicks contented himself with inscribing the date of his death and the Christian names of the deceased's parents, leaving the object and success of his travels a mystery to puzzle and embarrass posterity.

The city was thronged, on the morning Shah Soojah entered Caubul to resume his seat on the

---

* He must have been a stonemason, for it was beautifully carved.

throne of his ancestors, with the former adherents of Dost Mahomed, and many a scowl was bestowed on the Shah and his escort (consisting of a squadron of the 4th Dragoons, one of the 16th Lancers, and some Horse Artillery) as they wended their way through the streets, towards the palace, although none ventured to offer any insulting language to the conquerors of Afghanistan. The reception here was far different from that he had received at Kandahar, where he was little known. He passed in solemn silence through the bazaars, where, probably, but few spectators were present who had taken an active part in his deposition thirty years since ; yet tradition had handed down many a tale of oppression, and, regretting the mild and popular rule of Dost Mahomed, the inhabitants now submitted in silence to the evil they could not remedy. Such was the general impression conveyed by the demeanour of the soldiers and citizens ; but, obedient to the time-serving impulse which characterizes the venal soldiery of the two nations, both the Kuzzilbashes and Afghan cavalry flocked to tender their allegiance and services to the reinstated potentate. To the loyal and civilized inhabitants of the north this comparatively patient endurance of a change of masters may appear incredible ; but a perusal of the Afghan Dynasty will abundantly show that habit in this respect, as well as in many others, becomes a second nature. In the present instance, a considerable difficulty presented itself in the number of candidates for military employ; the revenue of the country being inadequate to maintain so large a force in addition to the numerous contingent which had been levied for the Shah in Hindostan. On the other hand, to reject the offers of these troublesome volunteers was tantamount to the distribution of an equal number of malcontents and robbers throughout Afghanistan, which was already abundantly supplied with these industrious communities. For the present, a great portion of the Kuzzilbashes were retained, and bodies of Afghan troops were shortly afterwards to be seen on the Champ-de-Mars of Caubul, practising, with laudable perseverance, the rigid miseries of the goose step.

A few days after our arrival the detachment which had been sent with Captain Outram, in pursuit of Dost Mahomed, returned from their laborious and unsuccessful chase. They had come within about twenty miles of the fugitive, who was accompanied by fifteen hundred Afghans, preferring to share the flight and dangers of Dost Mahomed to becoming renegades. Hadji Khan was nearly frantic with fear when he found the party had approached so much nearer the fugitives than he wished or intended. He entreated the British officers to abandon the pursuit, urging that their party was too small, and that not an Afghan of his retinue would raise a weapon against Dost Mahomed. This appears to have been one of the few truths he was known to utter, for the greater part of his retinue had already deserted. The party, however, in spite of all obstacles, strained every nerve to reach their object, but in the snowy fastnesses of the Hindoo Koosh these hardy mountaineers were not to be overcome, and the detachment was, at last, compelled to relinquish the pursuit and return to Caubul, where Hadji Khan was put in confinement, and afterwards sent as a prisoner to Hindostan.

Many are of opinion that Hadji Khan was harshly used by the Indian government, considering his ready adherence to the Shah on his arrival, and assert that, having openly abandoned his master, it became apparently his interest to secure his person. It is somewhat singular that, amongst a nation of renegades and traitors, any partiality should have been evinced in selecting an individual traitor, and one who, being influential, might have been made useful; whereas, if all had been convicted on suspicion, it would have been difficult to find conveyances and prisons for the state prisoners.

The Cavalry had now an opportunity offered them of replacing some of the horses which had been lost, for a very small number had been collected at Kandahar and Ghuzni.

Being on tolerably good terms with the Afghans, we were now able to see some of their best blood. The Government price for Cavalry remounts was restricted to four hundred and fifty rupees each horse, which was one hundred and fifty under the stud price, and the general opinion was in favour of the Caubul horse, when he could be found of sufficient size ; but, generally speaking, they were so well fattened up for the market that it required the eye of a good judge to detect faults under this general rotundity. The horse dealers were also found, in every respect, capable of competing with their brotherhood in England.

The only instance of an Afghan dealer being " done," which I saw or heard of, occurred on our march towards Caubul.

A dealer, one morning, came into the Cavalry lines, bringing a showy-looking nag for sale, which seemed a well bred animal, and certainly cocked its tail and pawed the ground in a most imposing manner. J . . . . , a young Dragoon officer, who was a very respectable jockey, asked the animal's price. " Fifteen hundred rupees," was the modest request ; " and you have not a sounder or fleeter animal in the Feringhee camp," added the Afghan. J . . . . quietly noticed one or two defects ; and pointing to a little old chesnut Arab, who certainly looked as if he were the ghost of some departed racer, but whose muscle and sinews only required the hand upon them to be acknowledged, offered to ride him a mile against the Afghan on his vaunted steed. The dealer eagerly closed the wager for a hundred rupees, and the ground was selected, as nearly as it could be guessed, for the distance. The riders were soon up, (the Afghan apparently the heavier;) the word was given, and away they went, the Afghan leading at a tearing pace, flourishing his legs and whip, and chuckling and hallooing with delight. J . . . . saw there was no necessity for collaring him, the Afghan doing all that could be desired. When within fifty yards of the winning-post, J . . ., having waited steadily on his competitor until the sleek animal was beat, gave the gallant little Arab his head and the Afghan the go-by, telling him to take his useless fifteen hundred rupees' worth home, as he had beaten him with the slowest horse in the regiment.

The fame of this race must have preceded the army, for I never heard another instance of an Afghan dealer wishing to match his horse for speed against any of our chargers. Their own races are generally for great distances, and the race-course is usually in the main road, where rocks and sharp stones are not scarce; but the horses are shod with a plate of steel which covers nearly the whole foot—a mode of shoeing adopted almost throughout the army. The Caubul ponies were very powerful and hardy animals, and have been much sought after and prized in Hindostan.

The Afghans do not appear to possess much attachment to their sovereign, though the feudal system prevalent would induce a contrary inference. Their merchandize fetching a favourable price, or the success of a marauding party, constitute their chief concernment; and the occupation of the musnud by a Barukzye, or Suddozye, is a matter of secondary importance to all, save, perhaps, the members of those two families, provided the people are unmolested in their avocations. In such a case, the usual practice has been to get rid of the obnoxious monarch as soon as a convenient conspiracy can be organized, which has been rarely unsuccessful. An escort, or pass, from a mountain-chief, will carry the bearer safely through that chief's territory ; but he must beware how he uses it beyond the assigned boundary, where it may prove worse than useless. Afghanistan is occupied by such a variety of tribes, each possessing their mountain fastnesses to retreat upon in case of need—men under no control beyond the temporary influence of their several leaders and chiefs—that it would certainly be an arduous undertaking to reduce the country to a complete state of subordination.

Under the different Shahs of Afghanistan, that portion of the people only who could be attracted and held by interested motives rallied round their king in times of trouble ; and amongst so capricious and disunited a people, the connecting link with their sovereign has always been weak, and often broken.

Whilst encamped in the vicinity of Caubul, a party of officers visited some hills about ten miles distant, under the escort of a petty mountain-chief, tributary to the Shah; the party were, of course, hospitably received by himself and the tribe, but his jurisdiction did not extend far. Pointing out the limits of his domain, he showed a dark range of hills, barely thirty miles' distant, belonging, as he said, to two chiefs, from whom Dost Mahomed had been unable to exact tribute or submission, although their dwellings were almost within sight of his palace-windows.

Even at this time, the British authority could not be said to extend beyond the chain of guards encircling our camp; for any soldiers or camp-followers straying far from the lines at night, and not unfrequently in the daytime also, stood a good chance of being shot, or cut down by some band of marauders. This hapless state of affairs remained unaltered during the whole time of our residence at Caubul.

Having been encamped for a fortnight, eight miles south of Caubul, the army were ordered to change ground to the north-eastern side, about two miles from the Bala Hissar, and on the Pe-shawur Road.

The day before moving, Brigadier Arnold (who had been suffering severely from illness since the army left Kandahar) died, universally regretted by the whole army, and especially by the 16th Lancers, which regiment he commanded, and to whom his loss was irreparable. We marched, in the even-ing, to the city; and the Lancers attended the remains of their colonel to the grave, which was dug at the foot of a steep, rocky mountain, about a quarter of a mile distant from the Bala Hissar. The funeral procession was attended by nearly all the officers of the army; and amongst them were few who had not experienced and appreciated the merits of that gallant soldier, who was now borne to the grave, from the effects of a bullet, which had pierced his breast when charging with the 10th Hussars at Waterloo.*

When the loose earth, which hides the tenement of the dead from the last sad gaze of the living, was cast on his coffin, the sullen roar of the cannon, which awakened from their reverie the abstracted group of mourners, and ran, telling their tale of woe, amongst the craggy precipices of the mountains of Caubul, found an echo of melancholy which thrilled in the hearts of his bereaved friends. I turned from the grave with the oppressive feeling of destitution which every soldier must experience on losing as gallant a colonel as ever drew a sabre, and as warm-hearted and accomplished a gentleman as even England can produce:

"Requiescat in pace."

---

* Colonel Arnold fell in the same charge, and with the same squadron, as Howard, the kinsman of Byron, immortalized in "Childe Harold."

Reports were in daily circulation that Dost Mahomed had crossed the Hindoo Koosh, and taken up his quarters with his brother-in-law, the King of Bokhara, who had promised his aid to the fugitive monarch in regaining the sovereignty, of which he had been deprived. Improbable as this was,—for had such been the intentions of the King of Bokhara, he would surely have advanced to the assistance of Dost Mahomed before his kingdom had been wrested from him,—Dr. Lord, of the political department, was sent with a military escort to cross the Indian Caucasus, and convey despatches, as well as gain intelligence, in that part of the country. The doctor had not reached Bameean, when, from the exaggerated reports of the inhabitants, he was led to suppose that Dost Mahomed, with a considerable force, was already between him and the mountain-pass. Not desiring a personal interview with the deposed Shah, whose arguments in favour of his own cause were likely to be weighty and incontrovertible, the political doctor wheeled about, and hastened to Caubul, where the intelligence induced Sir John Keane to order a force, under Colonel Sale, to be in readiness to move towards Bameean.

Two days after these orders were issued, news

arrived that Dost Mahomed, so far from crossing the Hindoo Koosh, was hastening in an opposite direction, with as much speed as the worthy doctor had used in his return to the capital. The force was consequently countermanded; and a detachment only, consisting of part of the Shah's goorkhas, and a few guns, were sent to occupy Bameean, which lies about eighty miles from Caubul, at the foot of the mountainous barrier, which divides Afghanistan from Bokhara. The road to this outpost was exceedingly bad; and even the small force of artillery which accompanied the party, delayed them nearly a fortnight, in crossing the rugged mountains and ravines which obstruct the road from Caubul to Bameean.

So much 1 aper has been already wasted on the Russo-phobia, that it would be superfluous to enter on a discussion of the obstacles which might oppose a march from the Caspian to the Indian Caucasus, over a country of which the little that is known has been gleaned from the scanty details of a few adventurous travellers, stealing in disguise over these inhospitable regions, and necessarily gleaning but meagre information. But of the difficulties which would present themselves to an army, on its arrival at the Hindoo Koosh, I think a very simple estimate may be formed.

The pass over those mountains, on account of its elevation, and the heavy falls of snow which constantly occur during the greater part of the year, is only practicable in the summer months, which would ensure the advantage of knowing at what time to expect an enemy. The road, by Herat, does not possess this advantage, being the easiest and most frequented passage into Afghanistan; but thence to Kandahar, the country possesses all the obstacles which opposed our progress through Lower Afghanistan, which would seriously affect a force whose strength and resources must have been materially weakened during a laborious march from the shores of the Caspian, even unopposed by an enemy. When arrived in the heart of Afghanistan, the greatest difficulties would oppose themselves to the maintenance of so numerous an army as would be requisite for so important an enterprise; and the palpable truth, that amongst these barren mountains a small army would be annihilated and a large one starved, must obtrude itself on the minds of all who are qualified to canvass the dilemma.

But an army which, by an effective commissariat and consummate fortune, advanced with its efficiency but little impaired, towards the frontiers of Hindostan, from the centre of Afghanistan, need not hastily congratulate itself on the charms of ultimate success, for the passages *out* of that country present as formidable barriers as the entrance *into* it, and these are the true outposts to the defensive frontier line of our Eastern Empire.

The intricate pass of the Kyber on the one side, and that of the Bolan, with the neighbouring Gundava, on the other frontier, being the sole outlets for an effective army,* form the natural outworks to the Indus, taken as a base of operations; and the policy which suggested the isolated position taken up in Afghanistan, with the far distant and imperfect lines of the Sutlej and lower Indus, was surely at variance with the admitted principles of military defence.

In either of the above-named passes, a small British force would maintain their ground against any odds; for the defiles being in many places not five yards in width, and flanked by craggy mountains which rise nearly perpendicularly on each side in many places, the numbers of the enemy would advantage him nothing, the heights

* The passes of Dera Ismael Khan, I have neglected to notice, as, after an active survey, they were reported impracticable for artillery.

K 3

being in our possession, whilst a strong palisade and battery, thrown across the road and covered by musketry from the adjacent heights, ought effectually to check his progress.*

That Russia *did* meditate hostilities in the East may be inferred from the detection of her envoy's intrigues at the courts of Persia and Caubul; but the reliance to be placed on the faith and promises of these agents may be fairly estimated from the observance of the following article in a treaty between the Shah of Persia and the Ameers of Kandahar.

Dated June, 1838.

ART. V. "If an enemy† should appear from any quarter, and the sirdars should not be able to repel him themselves, the Shah of Persia binds himself to supply the sirdars of Kandahar with troops, artillery, and money, to whatever extent may be necessary, and not to withhold any description of assistance or support."

The treaty, from which this article is extracted, was remitted to England by Dr. M'Neill. It is

---

* Had Dost Mahomed adopted these measures, it is probable Sir John Keane would never have obtained nobility.

† At this period, there could be little doubt who were the expected enemy, for Pottinger had proceeded, with a promise of assistance, to Herat.

thus countersigned by Count Simonich, the Russian agent:

"I, minister plenipotentiary* of the government of Russia, will be guarantee that neither on the part of H. M. &c. &c. &c., the Shah of Persia, nor on the part of the powerful† sirdars shall there arise any deviation from, or violation of, this entire treaty and their engagements.

(Signed) "L. S. Simonich."

Notwithstanding these promises of vigorous assistance from Persia, we had not the pleasure of meeting any portion of their armament in the vicinity of Kandahar, nor, to the best of our knowledge, were any Russian agents seen enforcing the Shah to perform Article No. V. of the above-named treaty. Yet an enemy did appear unto the sirdars of Kandahar, and from a quarter whence he had been many months expected, and those "powerful" chiefs did not even make the experiment of their ability to repel him.

Perhaps this article of the Shah's treaty was founded on the chance of the sirdars making the experiment; but, having adopted a more prudent course, there can be no doubt that a king, who

* Russia denies this big word.

† This irony is unbecoming the character of a plenipotentiary.

possesses so many sublime titles as the Shah of Persia, would not be guilty of a breach of faith; and therefore the Kandahar chiefs will speedily return from Persia with artillery, troops, and money, to an unlimited amount; in fact, sufficient (as the word " necessary," in the article quoted, must imply) to expel the British from Afghanistan; and, moreover, it is Count Simonich's duty to see this done. As Russia has disowned the threats, and the author met a conveniently political death, we may infer that the project of holding India with a chain of posts, stretching over mountains and deserts more than the semi-diameter of the globe in measurement, whilst the troublesome Dardanelles would materially interfere with all commercial intercourse, when watched by a British fleet, has been abandoned, and for the present a Russian invasion of India may be deemed improbable.

Although Afghanistan was now nominally subdued, the animosity and power of many mountain-tribes was unabated, and a few hours' ride from Caubul a cold blooded murder was committed on Colonel Herring, commanding a regiment of Native Infantry, on the march from Kandahar to join the army at Caubul. About forty miles from the capital, he strolled from camp in the evening, accompanied by two brother officers, with two sepoys in attendance. The party reached the summit of a hill, not more than a mile from the camp, when they descried a body of armed mountaineers advancing rapidly towards them. As the intention of the Afghans was evident, and their numbers considerable, Colonel Herring's party retired towards camp; but the assassins gained on them; and, in descending the hill, the Colonel, struck down by a stone or a matchlock ball, was immediately butchered. One of the sepoys, who was near Colonel Herring, in trying to defend him, was severely wounded, and left on the ground for dead. The regimental guard, on the alarm reaching the camp, hastened to the spot, but the miscreants had fled, after perpetrating their brutal outrage.

Shortly after the regiment's arrival at head quarters, Sir John Keane ordered a part of the 16th Native Infantry, under Major Maclaren, accompanied by some irregular horse, to scour the neighbourhood, and endeavour to ferret out the assassins. This object was successfully attained, and the indefatigable Maclaren, having traced them to a hill fort, assaulted and carried the place, when the garrison, conscious of fighting with halters round their necks, made a determined resistance, and were nearly all exterminated. This example had not the effect of restraining the bloodthirsty disposition of other bands of marauders; and the road between our camp and the city continued to be infested with assassins after nightfall. A dragoon was cut down, a night or two after, within a few yards of the standard guard, and similar instances were constantly occurring during our residence in the country. So expert were they at the practice, that retaliation could seldom be made. One instance I must relate, of a singular shot made by a soldier of a Dragoon regiment, who was skirting the hills, a few miles from camp, in pursuit of snipe and partridge, with a fowling piece loaded with small shot. He suddenly perceived an Afghan, forty paces from him, kneeling behind a rock, on which he had rested his matchlock, to make sure of his aim, and coolly waiting till his intended victim approached a little nearer. The soldier instantly threw the fowling-piece to his shoulder, fired, and rolled over his black game stone dead. A few shots had entered the brain and temples, and told with deadly haste.

As it was now considered improbable that any serious opposition to Shah Soojah's authority would be attempted, an order was issued, directing the Bombay column of the army of the Indus to return to their presidency by the route we had advanced.

On the 15th of September, 1839, our Bombay brethren quitted us, and proceeded on their homeward route, destroying, on their way, some petty hill forts, tenanted by refractory tribes. On approaching the fortress of Khelat, the residence of Mehrab Khan, whose duplicity had thrown such difficulties in our way by the promise of supplies, which were never sent, a deputation was forwarded to that chief, demanding atonement for his behaviour, and intimating, that nothing short of the most unqualified submission to Shah Soojah's clemency would avert the fall of his city and destruction of his power. Mehrab Khan preferred reposing confidence in the temper of his cimeter rather than in that of his sovereign; and General Willshire advanced upon Khelat with a brigade of infantry, consisting of her Majesty's 2nd and 17th regiments, and the 31stBengal Native Infantry, accompanied by a troop of horse artillery, and some irregular horse. The remainder of the column pursued their way towards the mountain-passes.

On approaching the fort, a large party of the

enemy, who held possession of the heights, opened their fire on the head of the British column. The enemy were soon dislodged from this post by the infantry; and, rushing from the heights into the city, were so closely pursued by their assailants, that the gates were shut barely soon enough to prevent the British from entering also. The troops, when falling back under cover from the galling fire which was now poured upon them from the walls of Khelat, lost several men.

Two horse artillery guns came up without delay, and their fire sufficed, in a few strokes, to crush the unprotected gate sufficiently to render an assault practicable. General Willshire now ordered the infantry to advance, which was hailed with the alacrity usual on similar occasions. With a cheer, they rushed up the ascent, regardless of the fire from the walls, and soon, beating down all opposition, took possession of the city. Mehrab Khan, surrounded by many of his chieftains and the greater part of the garrison, betook himself to the citadel, but this was incapable of defence; and the prince, with the greater part of his kinsmen and retinue, fell gallantly defending themselves at the gateway. Amongst the chief and his sirdars, no thoughts of surrender were harboured: each fought with a determination which put all chance of quarter out of the question; but the flashing cimeters of the Afghans, though wielded with the energy of desperation, soon drooped before the irresistible stroke of the British bayonet, which drank deeply that morning of the blood which, according to Colonel Mitchel, it never had, and never possibly could, shed.

When Mehrab Khan and his sirdars had fallen in the front of the struggle, the remainder of the garrison surrendered; and thus, under the prowess of British arms, fell the second important fortress of Afghanistan, and with a rapidity which, to the Afghans, must have been bewildering; for the bayonet glittered on the parapets of the citadel in less than two hours from the time it was levelled to drive the enemy on the heights under cover of the walls, which they fondly believed impregnable.

Such examples as had now been shown would, it was supposed, have taught the Afghans the vanity of resistance; but many revolting lessons of blood were yet requisite to teach these fierce mountaineers the necessity of submission, and our resolution of benefiting them, whether they wished it or not, with the inestimable advantages of civilization. But this radical reform can never be consummated in our day ; nor can I imagine a more arduous undertaking than such a crusade would be amongst a nation with whom the " lex fortioris" has been the established code of centuries.

The garrison of Khelat amounted to about two thousand men, as near as an estimate could be formed ; but the greater part of these fell during the storm.*

In General Willshire's force, which numbered about twelve hundred men, the casualties were— one lieutenant and thirty men killed ; four captains, four subalterns, and ninety-seven men wounded ; killed, Lieut. Gravatt, 2nd, or Queen's Regiment.

A great number of the wounded afterwards died before reaching Bombay, which induced a supposition of the enemies' weapons having been poisoned ; but there seems no foundation for the report. The climate below the mountain-passes was most probably the poison which carried off so many gallant fellows.

---

* The names of the chiefs who fell cannot be a matter of general interest; but those who have any curiosity on the subject, may find the list in General Willshire's despatch.

CHAPTER IX.

THE ARMY AT CAUBUL BROKEN UP — MARCH OF SIR JOHN KEANE'S ESCORT BY JELLALABAD, AND THROUGH THE KHYBER-PASS, TO PESHAWUR.

THE army of the Indus having effected the object for which they had been assembled, it was resolved to leave Shah Soojah to the charge of his loving subjects, supported by the contingent, and a small portion only of the force. The country being ill-adapted for cavalry, the news that the brigade, excepting one native regiment, were to be withdrawn, was received by the greater part with decided satisfaction; for many began to pine with regret at the protracted absence from their amiable halves; others were anxious to bind themselves in rosy (or thorny?) fetters; and, last and least, a few, after a long and painful estrangement, sighed deeply to participate once more in the pleasures of that deity, whose benign influence has been said to surpass " all that life can supply "—riches, love, ambition, friendship—

> " For what tongue will avow
> That friends, rosy wine, are so faithful as thou ?"

So wrote the virtuous and inconsistent Byron; and I have no doubt that a few habitual drunkards may concur in such an opinion.

The sole recommendation to Caubul was the temperate climate, which served to invigorate many who had severely felt the fatigues and exposure of this campaign, or who still suffered from the effects of their Indian enemy. To those who took pleasure in an active life and field-sports, our present quarters were irksome. The country possessed no attractions for the sportsman; and even in the pursuit of small game at any distance from camp, it was necessary to go prepared for more serious encounters; inasmuch as any straggler from the party stood an uncommonly good chance of being bagged by some Afghan huntsmen, whose sporting propensities led them to pursue white game with quite as much zest as ever, though, from the royal proclamation, it might be inferred that the season had closed.

Not satisfied with simply destroying their prey, these wild beasts mutilated the dead bodies, and arranged them in fanciful attitudes. Occasionally, a leg would be cut off, and placed under the head, for a pillow; the head itself would sometimes be found supported by the hands, in lieu of the neck; and I have seen things in a man's mouth which were never intended by nature to occupy such a situation.

To the antiquarian, Afghanistan presented some interest and employment in the collection of coins and antiques: many of the former were bought from the Afghans, bearing the names of the ancient Bactrian dynasty, and successors of Alexander the Great. The Afghans had, however, imbibed so great a taste for these antiquities, when they discovered the value we set upon them, that the manufacture and sale of the most ancient Bactrian coins is becoming a trade of some profit. Even at this day, both the Sikhs and Afghans converse with great interest on the feeble tradition they possess of events which occurred in the days of Shah Sikunder (Alexander the Great) and his generals, who subsequently governed this country. Alexander's Eastern expedition, the countries which he traversed, the localities of his engagements, and the modern names

of the nations with whom he fought, have been
much veiled in obscurity, owing to the very
slender knowledge possessed by Europeans of
the countries lying between Persia and Chinese
Tartary.

The numerous ancient coins and reliques,
monuments of Grecian design, the tradition of
the natives, and the names borne by many ancient
cities of Afghanistan and the Punjaub, (some of
which, at the present day, assimilate much to
those recorded by historians,) being matters of
recent discovery, will tend to assist the classic
labourer in such an investigation with materials
which have hitherto been wanting or imperfect.
As several officers who were with the army have
succeeded in making extensive collections of
ancient coins, I trust that, ere long, these may
tend to throw some light on the interesting subject. The evidence of Alexander's advance into
Hindostan, south of the Sutlej, is very vague,
especially as the princes of India made no attempt
to oppose his approach towards their frontier, as
the more warlike nations of Afghanistan and the
Punjaub undoubtedly did; and Porus, with his
herds of elephants, marks pretty accurately the
neighbourhood of the Hydaspes in the modern
Jelum, because the country north of Peshawur is

unfitted to nurture elephants. South of the Jelum or Hydaspes, I conceive the difficulty of tracing his route to be much greater, for the rivers are so numerous in the rainy season, and have changed their courses so materially, that the modern streams must differ considerably, both in number and position, from the ancient.

The accounts from the north of the Hindoo Koosh, about the beginning of October, showed the probability of a storm arising, ere long, in that quarter, directed by the hand of Dost Mahomed; and, in consequence, Sir John Keane ordered the whole of the Bengal infantry division to stand fast, for the present, in Afghanistan, for the security of Shah Soojah, who daily prophesied that our departure would be his death warrant.

The commander-in-chief himself, having resolved on returning to England, now signified in general orders, that on his departure the supreme command would devolve on Sir Willoughby Cotton.

The cavalry-brigade, (except the 2nd Native Cavalry, which was left in Afghanistan,) with a detachment of the European Regiment, and a few Sappers, formed the whole of the returning party escorting his excellency.

I little thought, at the time of quitting Bengal, that any fit of desperation could ever induce me to look forward with anything like pleasure to a residence in Hindostan; yet an experience of a few months' sojourn in the inhospitable and dreary wastes of Afghanistan proved that there were worse places on the face of this chequered globe than India.

Our retrospect, since leaving Merut, was not a very attractive one. Nearly a year had now been spent under canvas, or, more frequently, under the canopy of heaven, with a fierce sun scorching us unmercifully by day, and occasionally a damp chill to vary it by night. During the year, we had risen nearly every day about two or three hours before daybreak, and undergone the monotonous and wearisome marches, which resembled at last, in many respects, the morning's employment of a malefactor at the treadmill; and, to crown all, we had arrived at last in a country of rocks, savages, and starvation, where our chief occupation consisted in hunting continually for an enemy, who took care to deny us the excitement anticipated in the discovery. Such having been, with trifling exceptions, the result of our campaign, every source of employment, beyond that above mentioned, was confined to the narrow limits of a little canvas world, peopled almost entirely by the grosser sex of black and white; for the small portion of the opposite sex and former colour who sojourned amongst us, were scarcely attractive enough to remind one of the generic distinction which existed. To these hardships, and others in addition, we would more cheerfully have submitted, had an enemy kept us on the alert, and played, on an extensive board, the rough game of war; but the only enemies we had met were scarcely deserving such a name—ensconcing themselves behind mud walls, or perched on inaccessible heights—and as there appeared now little chance of tilting with the Afghan clans in the open field, it was with feelings of pleasure we looked forward to an emancipation from the barren mountains of Afghanistan.

The Punjaub was, at this period, in so distracted a state, that the government of the country betrayed a marked anxiety that we should not become witnesses of their anarchy and disunion. Even in the days of Runjeet Singh, the Sikhs beheld with feelings of uneasiness the advance and establishment of the British outposts on the Sutlej; and the passage of troops through their country caused even greater jealousy and alarm, for they considered, not perhaps without some foundation, from a few precedents in the East, that when the English had once got a footing, they might take a fancy to remain there.

In the present crisis of affairs, it was apprehended that these Sikh scruples would act as a temporary obstacle to our departure; but, fortunately for us, the court of Lahore yielded a reluctant assent to our passing through their country, and on the morning of the 15th of Oct. we quitted Caubul.

The breaking up of a long-standing camp is a scene of no trifling bustle and confusion. The previous day is usually one of considerable trouble to those who have suffered their marching-establishment to get out of order; and when it is requisite to replace a camel or a bullock, the new comer, even if found, (and that is generally at a ruinous price,) not unfrequently evinces the most marked repugnance to tents or bullock-trunks. Yet, however great the difficulty, the peremptory necessity of the habitation being moved before next morning, causes all to be prepared at sunset, either by a reduction of baggage, or increase of cattle, save the more provident campaigners, who rectify such deficiencies without delay. The earliest practicable hours are kept by all off duty, and two hours after sunset

the camp (if well regulated) is quiet enough, unless a horse breaks loose and sets the whole
brigade in a state of ferment; for all seem to take
a deep interest in the progress of any mad animal
who tears through the camp, with ropes and pegs
flying in wild confusion about his heels. As night
advances, even these stray madcaps betake themselves to rest, and the quiet is only disturbed by
the hourly tramp of patrols, or the challenge of a
sentry. This gloom and stillness are suddenly
dissipated by the shrill startling blast of the
trumpet, wakening all around to consciousness
and activity. The loud and continued neigh
from the pickets, and the angry remonstrances of
the camels, amidst the extensive buzz of human
voices and barking of dogs, tell that man and
brute are both aware of the time having come
for their allotted duties. Sticks and dry grass
raked into pyramids are sending forth volumes of
smoke in one place, and in another are rising
into high crackling fires, round which may be
seen groups of dusky figures squatted together,
inhaling their morning hookahs, or spreading
their long bony hands to the flames, and listlessly
regarding their more assiduous brethren occupied
in striking the tents, or fitting loads on the backs
of the beasts of burden. But think not, my lazy

fire - worshipper, this indolence is unobserved; the eye of the occupant of yonder tent is upon you: he advances softly towards the fire, his arm is raised, and the descending lâttie causes a momentary scene of flight and confusion which is immediately succeeded by a zealous attention to duty, proving the salutary force of the " Argumentum ad baculum." Although this is not an orthodox, logical, or even legal argument, it is, nevertheless, frequently used in India, and is generally conclusive. Next morning, the voice, unaccompanied by manual exercise, will produce the desired effect.

The loads being packed, and all the tents, save three or four lazy stragglers, having disappeared, the second trumpet sends its shrill echoes through the lines, and gives warning that the treadmill will soon be at work. Beware of that camel's mouth gaping close to your hand in the dark, or he will spoil it for holding a rein or a sabre; and beware the treacherous tent-peg, which lurks in savage gloom for the shins of the unwary. " It is no use cursing the peg. Why did you not get out of its way when you found it was not inclined to get out of yours ?" cries a facetious neighbour, as you stoop to rub the lacerated shin, and narrowly escape being trampled by an elephant, who is hustling off with a few hundred weight of canvas and tent-poles hanging about him.

The third trumpet and a cup of *boiling* coffee generally accompany each other, if your khansanah belong to the right Dean Swift's breed; and it is no punishment to insist on his drinking it himself—the man would swallow a cup of cayenne and fire, without winking.

The troops are formed in dusky masses on their alarm-posts; the commanding-officer rides along the line; the word of command is given, and passed down the squadrons; the welcome note for the march is heard, and the tramping of the steeds raises an impenetrable cloud of dust around the column, as we cheerfully turn our backs on Caubul, most probably for ever; the band prophetically striking up, "Ha til mi tulidh," or something which I mistook for it.

Sir John Keane marched with the head column, consisting of the 16th Lancers, one troop of Horse Artillery, and four companies of Native Infantry. General Thackwell followed, the next day, with the 3rd Native Cavalry, detachments of Infantry, and the state prisoners, Hyder Khan, late governor of Ghuzni, and Hadji Khan Kaukur. The former was destined for Bombay, the latter, for Bengal, where it was intended to place him in close confinement at Chunar, on the Ganges; but this was afterwards commuted for a more salutary and agreeable durance at Landour, where Hadji Khan had little cause to complain of the severity of his captors.

The 2nd Bengal Cavalry, which were left at Caubul, soon afterwards had an opportunity of distinguishing themselves at Purwan Durrah, in an encounter with Dost Mahomed. The Ameer having been nearly surrounded by his enemies, and entertaining a low opinion of the courage of the Native Cavalry, resolved to dash through the circle at the post held by the above-named corps, and accompanied by a determined body of his adherents, he charged two squadrons of the 2nd Cavalry.

The officers of the regiment having tried unsuccessfully to induce their men to follow, formed a line, and gallantly charged the Afghan force. Three of the regiment were killed, and most of the remainder severely wounded; but such was the moral effect of this behaviour, that Dost Mahomed exclaimed, " that war against such a nation must be hopeless."

The dastardly black fugitives who had been spectators, during their flight, of the self-devotion and butchery of their officers, spread themselves in the wildest disorder and affright, but the avenging cimeters of the Afghans soon flashed amongst them, and dealt a partial retribution for their detestable cowardice.

The number of this regiment was afterwards erased from the list of the Company's troops, and the corps was disbanded at Kurnaul, with the exception of one squadron, which, not having been present at Purwan Durrah, was distributed throughout the remaining regiments of Native Cavalry. The officers were provided with various situations in the Company's service, and subsequently incorporated in a new cavalry regiment, (the 11th.)

Some attempts to palliate the conduct of the 2nd Cavalry, on this occasion, have been attempted; and I have heard it adduced in extenuation, that the men (save the mark!) had no confidence in their arms and equipments or their *horses bits*— that they reverenced Dost Mahomed and the Afghans as the heads of their religion*—and that British cavalry have also been known to be backward.

Regarding the first of these assertions, we need but ask—Is not the Native Cavalry soldier as carefully instructed in the use of his weapon as

* Most of the Company's cavalry regiments are composed of Mussulmans.

the English Dragoon? If he be, there is no
reason for his running away. If he be not, I
cannot admit that a brave man is likely to run
away with a piece of English steel in his hands,
because he thinks he is not sufficiently instructed
in the use of the sabre, or because he prefers
Hindustanee manufacture.

In answer to the second apology, it is only
requisite to state, that if they did respect the
Afghans as brother Mussulmans, experience
should long before have taught them that the
feeling was by no means mutual. The irregular
horse were affected with no such compunctions,
but evinced a laudable desire to destroy their
enemies, when called upon to do so, on several
occasions, in Afghanistan.

To the third charge, I must plead guilty of ignorance; for I cannot remember having heard or
read of any British cavalry regiment absconding
in the face of an enemy, and leaving their officers
to charge, unaided by a single trooper of the
corps.*

On quitting our camp at Caubul, we marched
over a rough and stony road for about ten miles,

* A few days after this skirmish, Dost Mahomed surrendered himself to the envoy, and was sent a prisoner to Hindostan.

and encamped on some high grounds. In the afternoon, we experienced a smart shock of an earthquake here, which appeared to come rumbling towards us from the mountains of the Hindoo Koosh, and upset nearly everything in our tents. From the elevated ground on which we were encamped, we had a farewell view of Caubul and the noble chain of the Indian Caucasus, still clad in bright snowy garments.

The next morning, we entered a steep, rocky* pass, between two ranges of mountains, where the cold before sunrise was intense, and the aspect certainly the most dreary we had hitherto experienced. We emerged, half frozen, from this stony sepulchre, and gladly thawed ourselves in the sun, which shone dimly on the platform of rock where our camp was pitched.

Each day, as we advanced, the roads (if they can be deemed worthy such a title) became decidedly worse. Our third day's march lay through another narrow defile, across which dashed several rapid mountain torrents at intervals of about a mile from each other. The next day's occupation was a steep rocky ascent, and

---

* This was the pass of Khoord Caubul, afterwards memorable in General Elphinstone's final retreat from Caubul.

an equally sudden fall, which caused a corresponding one with our unfortunate beasts of burden.

A succession of deep, stony ravines, and occasionally sharp-pointed rocks, presented the next variety.

On the 7th of March, we wound up a long gradual ascent of some twelve or fourteen miles, and on descending from this elevation two guns were discovered not far off the road, embedded in the sand. These had been abandoned here by Dost Mahomed's son, (Mahomed Akbar,) when retreating from the gorge of the Khyber to join his father previous to their flight from Urghundee.

On the eighth march from Caubul, we descended into the celebrated valley of Neemla, where Shah Soojah had been finally defeated in 1809, and expelled from his kingdom. It is a small, well-cultivated valley, surrounded by barren, craggy mountains, (as is the case, indeed, with almost every valley in the country.) If the numbers present at this battle are correctly stated, it must have been a business of tolerably close quarters, and little scope could have been afforded for manœuvring: but the Afghans are not much addicted to wasting time in military operations. A favourite mode of attack is the chupao, or surprise by night, (which was practised at Neemla,) and if the enemy be found prepared, or the first charge prove unsuccessful, they prefer reserving their energies for a more favourable opportunity, to pressing the matter any further under such critical circumstances as a spirited resistance might entail. The party making the night attack certainly act under the more favourable circumstances of the two, as in case of failure a retreat is open under cover of the darkness, and unmolested; whereas, the party attacked once getting into disorder, can scarcely hope to rally under such disadvantageous circumstances. Thus it was at the battle, or, rather, the route of Neemla, where Shah Soojah was encamped, with a force exceeding fifteen thousand men, whilst his adversary, with barely two thousand fighting men, coming down suddenly during the night, took the Shah so completely by surprise, that he forthwith devoted all his attention to preserve his own royal person, leaving his army to do all the fighting part without any general. Of course they soon got into hopeless confusion, and followed the example of their prudent master before the chiefs were able to marshal their numerous forces. Such are the chances and vicissitudes of war.

Want of timely information, a picket ill posted, or a vidette falling asleep, may cause the loss of an army and an empire.

The tenth march from Caubul brought us to the green and lively-looking valley which contains Jellalabad, and the march between this and Caubul, which we had now happily overcome, was unanimously allowed to be the worst we had experienced. Our camels had certainly great cause to complain, and they neglected not to do so; but man and beast endured much on this march—the former a pecuniary, the latter a bodily suffering—let naturalists decide which endured the heavier affliction.

Jellalabad* is an insignificant place of itself, though situated in a fertile valley, through which rolls the clear Caubul river, washing the foundations of the city walls, and they certainly required no impotent scavenger. It has been selected as a residence by the kings of Caubul for the winter season, owing to the mildness of the climate, from its depressed situation, (about two thousand feet above the sea;) and this recommendation induced the commander-in-chief to select it as winter quarters for the greater portion of the army

* The well-known site of Sir Robert Sale's gallant defence.

remaining in Caubul during the ensuing cold season.

According to the prevalent opinion, Jellalabad lays claim to considerable antiquity, as it has been supposed to represent the site of ancient Nysa. Numerous copper coins, as well as some curious antiques, have been from time to time collected in the vicinity of this place by the natives. Unfortunately, nearly all the gold and silver coins and reliques have been melted down, as the natives themselves admitted, and converted into bangles, nose-and-ear rings, or other ornaments, for the dusky beauties of Jellalabad. Several copper coins, bearing the name of Hermæus, king of Nysa, distinctly legible, were bought amongst the country people. The inscription was in Greek letters, and as follows:

ΒΑΣΙΛΕΟΣ ΕΡΜΑΙΟΥ ΣΩΤΗΡΟΣ.

Those of the Bactrian monarchs found in different parts of the country are also in Greek; and the figures and hieroglyphics on the coins have been converted, by erudite conjectures, into an endless variety of meanings. Heaven, earth, and sea have been ransacked to discover the symbolical allusions on a piece of grangrened copper; and the half-effaced toes of a Bactrian savage

were successively mistaken for the signs of the
Zodiac, the trident of Neptune, and a Barbarian
coronet.* By dint of much cleansing, the toes
became apparent, then appeared the legs; and
over them, the body and intellectual countenance
of the tiresome Hermæus shone conspicuous, with
a well-flattened nose, and a pair of monstrous
eyes, one of which seemed to leer with a knowing expression of cunning on his indefatigable
polishers.

Near Jellalabad, we found encamped some of
Runjeet's Mussulman troops, which had accompanied Colonel Wade through the Khyber Pass,
about three months previously, when that distinguished officer advanced upon Ali Musjid, and
opened his batteries on that remarkable fortress.
The siege was conducted with such vigour, and
so severe was the effect of the cannonade, that
the loss on the part of the besieged must have
been very serious, although the exact number of
the sufferers could not be ascertained. Colonel
Wade's losses, in killed and wounded, during the
investment, amounted to something less than two
hundred, which was about the strength of half
the garrison.

* The coin which caused so much trouble and conjecture
is now in my possession.

In the course of the first night after the investment of Ali Musjid, intelligence reached the garrison of the fall of Ghuzni, and of the return of
Mahomed Akbar with his forces from the mouth
of the Khyber towards Caubul. This news, it is
supposed, coupled with the *incalculable* losses of
the previous day, induced the Khyberees to evacuate Ali Musjid during the night. Next day, the
fortress was joyfully taken possession of by Col.
Wade; and that celebrated despatch was penned
which informed Lord Auckland and the people of
India that, in consequence of " The capture of
Ali Musjid, and the successful advance of the
British forces into Afghanistan, there remained
no doubt of the speedy dethronement of Dost
Mahomed, and the favourable issue of the Afghan
campaign."

Having quitted Jellalabad, we proceeded along
the banks of the Caubul river, which is here
skirted for some distance by a stony plain, over
which the deadly simoom is said to be an occasional traveller during the hot season. Five
marches from Jellalabad brought us to the gorge
of the formidable Khyber Pass, the position occupied by Mahomed Akbar at the opening of the
campaign. The mountains through which this
defile runs are inhabited by the Khyberees, a

tribe who have from time immemorial exacted
tribute of all passengers through their gloomy
mountains, and Dost Mahomed himself considered
it politic to pay them annually a large sum to
keep open the pass for traffic, as well as to secure
so formidable a barrier against any sudden freak
of his hereditary enemies in the Punjaub. These
troublesome mountaineers also succeeded in ex-
acting contributions from the inhabitants of the
Peshawur district, in payment for a stream of
water which issued from the Khyber mountains,
and supplied the frontier position of the Sikhs at
Futtehghur.

Colonel Wade, in his passage through this
defile, endeavoured to treat with the chiefs of
the Khyberees; and even bribed some of them,
by a considerable bonus, to ensure a free passage; but, subsequently, so many presented themselves to demand bribes, that the negotiation bade
fair to become expensive, and it was evident that
this hydra was more amenable to steel than gold.

Many of the chiefs had expected payment, for
the use of their productive mountains, on the
return of the army through the Khyber pass, but
part of Colonel Wade's force had returned, and
no bribes for the chieftains had accompanied them.
The Khyberees, therefore, were much exasperated

at the prospect of a failure of revenue ; and, fearing that if once the precedent of passing freely through their mountains were established by the British, their black mail might henceforth be reduced to a cipher, they vowed vengeance on the first intruders, and had now an opportunity of trying the experiment.

The entrance of the Khyber much resembles that of the Bolan pass, except that the footing was the same as on a beach of shingles in the former, and in the latter a platform of rock. On our flanks rose abrupt rocks, during the first day's march, untenanted by animal or vegetable; barrenness held undisputed rule.

On the second day, we ascended a steep mountain by a path resembling those cut on the Missourie and Landour range, and, descending by a similar road of about ten feet in breadth and occasionally less, entered a valley of some extent, sprinkled with several little villages and some melancholy grainfields. Traversing this valley, we entered a narrow, rocky defile, and following the course of a mountain torrent by its narrow passage through the beetling rocks, arrived, unmolested by the Khyberees, at Ali Musjid, after a march of about fifteen miles.

This fort, which stands on a steep hill about

three hundred yards from the gorge of the stony defile above mentioned, had been occupied, since Colonel Wade's departure, by an officer of Native Infantry with a levy of Mooltanee recruits and a few sepoys. During the summer, the place had been found so extremely unhealthy that a great portion of the garrison died, and most of those who escaped were left in a very weak state. Inside the fort itself there is no water, and this useful article was brought by the garrison from a water-course and well, about three hundred yards distant from the walls. As there were no cannon in this formidable place, the possession of the water-course became very precarious in case of the enemy attempting to cut off the communication. The Khyberees, well aware of these disadvantages, came down, latterly, nearly every night to attack the place; but were gallantly repulsed by the little garrison as often as they came, and frequently with considerable loss. Five days before our arrival, a regiment of Sikhs, from Peshawur, amounting to nearly eight hundred, although many were in a sickly state, had occupied a small stockade,* on an eminence, about one mile distant from Ali Musjid, for the garrison of which place they had brought supplies.

* The stockades are made of loose stones and beams.

During the night, this regiment was suddenly attacked by a force of about two thousand Khyberees. The Sikhs defended themselves within their stockade for above an hour, when their ammunition being spent, and the enemy still pressing hard upon them, they quitted their entrenchments in the hopes of effecting a retreat upon Ali Musjid. No sooner had the unhappy men evacuated their stronghold than they were surrounded by their merciless foes, and nearly the whole regiment was destroyed. Not twenty men, it was believed, escaped to bear these disastrous tidings to Peshawur. The little garrison in Ali Musjid had been effectually prevented from attempting a diversion in favour of their unfortunate allies, by a force of Khyberees, which were stationed so as to intercept the communication between the fort and the stockade. Had any part of the garrison, under such circumstances, quitted Ali Musjid, they must inevitably have been overwhelmed by the Khyberees, and in the darkness of night would, in all probability, have shared the fate of the Sikhs; but no doubt was entertained in Ali Musjid that the stockade would make good its defence.

We arrived late in the afternoon, and encamped by this field of recent slaughter, which presented a dreary spectacle; the effluvia arising from the half buried bodies and limbs of the Sikhs was almost poisonous, though it seemed to give no inconvenience or nausea to the Pariah dogs and vultures who were enjoying the ample repast provided for them by and upon the lords of the creation.

An attack on our camp being anticipated at this place, orders were issued, prohibiting both officers and men from quitting the lines, and a chain of sentries were posted, in the evening, on the summit of the lower range of hills which encircled our camp.

None of my baggage having made its appearance at nightfall, I fully made up my mind to the loss of such part of the wreck as remained, and seated myself, for the night, on a rock, where, having loaded my pistols in anticipation of the Khyberees' visit, I awaited that important event.

It was a bright starlight night. All in camp were hushed in sleep, save the guardians of the lines, who testified their vigilance by striking the hours on a lugubrious sounding gong, or by the ringing of their arms as the patrols or reliefs traversed the encampment.

As I sat in contemplation of the still scene around me, the solemn thought occurred that in a very few hours, this deathlike stillness might be locked in that sleep to be disturbed only by the sound of the last trumpet. That band of eight hundred Sikhs, which lay here but five nights past, slept on, in all probability, (until aroused by the war notes of the Khyberees,) with the same careless security that my fellow-soldiers were now enjoying, and they awoke to be slain, in one short hour—

> "A thing
> O'er which the raven flaps her fun'ral wing."

It is a strange sensation that interview which we are constrained to hold with death; yet, with all the imaginary terrors in which he is clad, the brave man readily meets him face to face. That those only who are, morally speaking, prepared to die, fear not death, is too wild a theory to be maintained: for many of us have seen the hardened malefactor advance, with unfaltering step and fearless aspect, to the scaffold, while in the ranks of the timid have been numbered some of the best of mankind.

And my fellow-countrymen here, who have, at least, been educated in the constant hearing of the word of God—are they more fitted to die than those miserable heathens were, whose carcases are now tainting the atmosphere? Let those who are more competent to judge of such matters decide. We, who, according to the declaration of our divines and the boast of government, are sent out to retain possession of this vast country, and to exhibit to the benighted natives the benefits and example of Christianity, have performed the latter part of our ministry in a singular manner, unless it is to be effected by daily instances of blasphemy, drunkenness, and debauchery, that the natives of India are enabled to witness. And yet they have been inapt scholars, for we have failed signally in propagating amongst them the two former accomplishments, and I question much if they have excelled us in the latter. And yet let it not be imputed to us that we are the only, or the greatest, transgressors. Let the traveller who has wandered through the bazaars of Cairo, Bombay, Caubul, Delhi, or Canton, and marked the character and occupation of the Mussulman, Gheber, and idolator, compare them with the gin palaces, cafés, bull fights, and gardens or thoroughfares of London, Paris, Madrid, Vienna, and Naples, and exult (if candour will admit) in the moral advantages of civilized Europe. I ask him not to visit the palaces of the aristocracy, or the church and chapel; in the former he will gain no knowledge, and in the latter, perhaps, too much; for, of all sciences, theology has become the most abstruse; and he who can recognise the immaculate precepts of Jesus of Nazareth, amidst the fiery and relentless hostilities of modern sects, must be an unhappy man. For my own part, the nice distinctions of party in the early history of the church, the difficulty of deciding between the mighty and learned differences of the Christian fathers, and the inability to distinguish between the Homoosion and the Homouosion quite disheartened me, at the outset, in the study of divinity; and in modern days the fiery animosities of catholic and protestant, transubstantiation, predestination, the gown and surplice riot, and pulpit mendicity, drove me from the church portals to take refuge in the book.

But, after this peregrination of the globe, to return to India: is it by the example of the better-educated classes, and the stern and impartial dealing of justice, that the natives of the East are to form an estimate of our superior wisdom and excellence? If so, let them look to some in the high places of this land, and be staggered at the display of erudition, wisdom, and righteousness; and let them judge of our notions of rigorous justice from the policy which dictated the expedition from which we are now returning.

Have we not marched into the kingdom of Caubul, and without any pretext or right, save the " lex fortioris," wrested the sceptre from the hands of one monarch, the favourite of his subjects, as far as any Afghan could be so, to transfer it to those of another, (and one avowedly of a tyrannous and execrable disposition,) after shedding the blood of those who stepped forward in defence of him whom they probably conceived to be their rightful sovereign? It can hardly be assumed that the desire of establishing legitimate rights led us romantically forth on the Caubul expedition; for the government of India held friendly intercourse with Dost Mahomed for many years, without questioning his sovereign rights, and only discovered how ill-used a man Shah Soojah had been, when Dost Mahomed showed a disinclination to enter into hostilities with those who were deemed to be averse to British influence.

I had just come to the above conclusion, when a tramping behind aroused me from my reverie; and starting up, I was agreeably surprised to find that all my camels and servants had walked safely into camp. I rolled myself in a cloak, and making a comfortable resting-place of the folds of canvas composing the fly of the tent, soon became insensible alike to the immoralities of mankind and the intentions of the Khyberees.

The morning sun, when I awoke, had burst brilliantly forth, even upon the desolate and gloomy mountains of the Khyber, trying, but in vain, to bid them look cheerful; and the night, contrary to all expectations, had passed without an alarm. In the afternoon, the second column, under General Thackwell, arrived at Ali Musjid; and orders were issued for our march out of the Khyber Pass the following morning. In consequence of the reports which had reached camp of the intention of the Khyberees to attack us, the two companies of sappers and miners formed our advanced guard, and the cavalry were disposed in single files on the flanks of the baggage, with a rallying-party from each squadron in rear, as a point of formation in case of a descent from the mountains.

We marched, at daybreak, along the rugged course of a torrent, which had now degenerated to a shallow, trickling stream. High, barren mountains beetled above and almost over our track; and frequently their bases approached so near to one another, that six could scarcely ride abreast. At every step, we expected to see our enemies make their appearance on the heights, from whence they might almost with impunity have done us any injury which their long rifles, or juzzails, were capable of inflicting; but, singularly enough, not an enemy was to be seen, and we passed unmolested through the rugged defile. At about six miles from the outlet, we encountered a large body of Sikh troops occupying the road, whilst detachments were posted above them on the heights. These belonged to the army of the frontier, stationed at Peshawur. With their national modesty, they failed not to inform us that they were our deliverers from the hands of the Khyberees; and loudly proclaimed, that without their co-operation, we never should have escaped from the jaws of the Khyber Pass. Nevertheless, these heroes had taken the precaution of not advancing into the most arduous part of the defile; and previously to the British advance into Afghanistan, they had not been much acquainted with the geography of these mountains.

Towards the exit of the Pass, the mountains, though loftier and nearly as abrupt, recede considerably from one another. On emerging from them, we entered an extensive plain, and encamped near the fort of Futtehghur, which was lately built by Runjeet Singh as a frontier position. Near its walls, a long line of dusky tents marked the station of the Peshawur forces. Our lines were soon overrun by swarms of inquisitive Sikh warriors, mounted on lean, weedy horses, and carrying lances and beards of nearly equal length.

We marched early the following morning. The ground we quitted was soon occupied by the rear column, which also passed unobstructed through the defile with the state-prisoners.

The Sikhs raised a yell of execration and abuse at the sight of Hadji Khan; but he, turning in his saddle with a smile of contempt, exclaimed—

" Yelp on, ye dastardly curs—it was not *your* prowess which made me a captive! Many a time, at the head of a few brave Afghan followers, have I made ye sing a different song; and, with Allah's help, I trust I may live to do so again!"

On the morning of the 7th of November, we crossed the rich valley of Peshawur, and approached the city, having bidden adieu to the rocks and deserts of Afghanistan without a single regret, and with the fervent hope of never revisiting the realms of our ally, Shah Soojah.

CHAPTER X.

THE approaches to the city from the north-east are commanded by a large fort, recently completed by the assistance of some French officers, and under the eye of General Avitabilè.

The fort is surrounded by a dry ditch, and constructed on modern principles of fortification, but placed in such convenient proximity to the city, as to obviate the necessity of opening trenches and labouring at parallels in case of a siege. Passing immediately under this stronghold, we wound along the outside of the low mud-walls which surround Peshawur, and encamped on its Eastern front. The city seemed of enormous extent, and contained, as we were told, more than twelve thousand houses within its walls; but certainly the greater part of them were better adapted for pigsties than dwelling-houses.

The government of this district was in the hands of General Avitabilè, an Italian officer, who had served for a long time under Runjeet Singh, and had been raised by him to distinction and wealth. His government, although severe, was generally allowed to have kept the savage neighbours of the adjacent mountains in more terror and subjection than any former governor was enabled to attain. According to Runjeet's code, no capital punishment was inflicted on the Sikhs by law; but this was in no way applicable to the marauders dwelling in the hills which border Peshawur, on whom, as well as over the Mussulman population of Peshawur, the governor occasionally endeavoured to make up for Runjeet's misplaced leniency. Numerous examples of punishment were presented to our view near the city walls on the high palm-trees, to which were appended strings of such acorns as Trois Echelles and Petit Andre loved to adorn the oaks of Plessis les Tours with in the days of Louis Onze. On every side of the city, were seen well-furnished gibbets, or frail and wasted relics of humanity, strung upon beams, nailed between the blighted palms. Those who had recently been promoted to their exalted situations were favourites with the kites and vultures, whose discordant screams of health and prosperity to Governor Avitabilè, whilst circling round their hideous repast, were gloomily answered by the rattling and clatter of some well-picked skeletons, as they swung to and fro in the evening blast. Disgusting as these objects seemed, we must nevertheless, according to the opinion and quotation of an American traveller, hail them as testimonies of civilization. If an appeal to the worst passions of mankind be a test of civilization, Mr. Willis is in the right; but I confess I have felt much more gratified in seeing a rude and uneducated Hindoo turn with loathing from the execution of a criminal about to be blown from a cannon than I have at the exhibition of thousands of my countrymen struggling for places, and paying high prices for seats, to witness the protracted, dying struggles of a malefactor and fellow-sinner.

In Afghanistan, no sooner is the light applied to the touchhole of the cannon,* than the limbs of the victims are distributed to the winds of

* This mode of execution has also been practised by the princes of many independent states of Hindostan.

heaven; but in England, in Christian England, where societies for preventing cruelty to animals have been established, and rewards offered for the speediest method of ending the sufferings of beasts, the agonies and struggles of a fellow-creature, whilst undergoing a death, (which, according to the letter of the law, is not expected to be instantaneous,*) are deemed a fit subject for the entertainment of the multitude; for it is notorious that Englishmen prefer attending an execution to any other resort of public amusement. Yet this disgusting spectacle, this barbarous relic of despotic authority, is to be exhibited and justified solely on the plea of example. I cannot bring myself to believe that one solitary mortal was ever deterred from committing a murder by the fact of his having witnessed a public execution; whereas the very notoriety has been known to excite men to earn the vile publicity.

At Peshawur, the systematic method of suspen-

* In 1842 I witnessed a military execution at Merut, of a private of the Horse Artillery. The numerous spectators present can bear witness to the prolonged sufferings of the criminal. The rope being adjusted, one native pushed him off a low cart under the gibbet, whilst two others tugged at the rope to hoist him up. The convulsive writhings of the sufferer long haunted me; they lasted for nearly twenty minutes.

sion *by the neck* was not universally adopted, for the fancy of the executioner was occasionally shown by a varied figure of victims suspended alternately by the head and heels. At Peshawur, also, has been revived the nearly obsolete, but classical, punishment of skinning alive. The executioner begins this operation by raising the skin on the soles of the feet, which is then torn in strips upwards, and the wretched creature is left vainly to wish for the relief which death sometimes does not afford within two hours of the infliction.

Cutting off the arms and legs, and steeping the stumps in hot oil, putting out the eyes, or docking the ears of the culprits, are the milder corrections for minor delinquencies.

I shall not attempt to deny that the daring atrocities which have been perpetrated require to be restrained with a strong hand, and punished with death, but the protraction of suffering cannot, I think, be exculpated. If life must be taken, let it be done without parade or procession, and, above all, let it be instantaneous.

On the evening of our arrival, the governor entertained the officers of the first column with a banquet and fête, at his palace in Peshawur. The edifice and gardens glittered with brilliant illuminations, and a splendid display of fireworks was the prelude to the banquet. The table groaned under a weight of food which far surpassed in quantity any accumulation of the kind of which I have partaken; but, alas, I must confess my utter ignorance of the vocabulary of the cuisine; and though I was fortunate enough to sit by the side of a man who enumerated every dish, and dignified some with very uncommon names, I was too absent or too stupid to remember them.

Many complained of the want of recherche of his cook; but possibly he conceived that, after the experience we had recently had of scarce and coarse fare, dainties and the more abstruse arts of cookery would have been wasted upon us. For my own part, I confess that the paraphernalia of the surrounding gibbets haunted me so much at the table that I could hardly take my eyes off an immense cone of rice, piled on a huge dish in front of the master of the feast, and as the snowy covering was shaken off, I could scarcely persuade myself that the boiled kid and trussed-up capons were not some novel delicacies artistically carved from a skinned criminal!

The feast being ended, we were ushered into a room above-stairs, where a circle of Nautch girls were squatted round the room, who entertained us with a repetition of those monotonous chants and attitudes which are so generally popular amongst the Orientals.

Some of the women, especially the Punjaubees, were pretty: all had fine lustrous eyes, and some fair and almost clear olive complexions; but cocoa-nut oil, beetel nut, vermillion, henna, and black paint, did their utmost to detract from the gifts of Nature. However, we had been so long debarred from the sight of female charms, that few had any reason to be fastidious or backward in admiration of such novelties, and none of the damsels reckoned shyness or obstinacy as accomplishments.

On the morning of the 10th of November, the Sappers and Miners, and two companies of Native Infantry, were detached to Ali Musjid in the Khyber pass, as an escort to a quantity of camel-loads of supplies of provision and ammunition for the use of the garrison. Having performed this duty, on their return from Ali Musjid they were suddenly attacked by a swarm of Khyberees. A party of Sikhs who accompanied the detachment, either from treachery or fear, at the first alarm severed the leading-strings of the camels, and thus threw the baggage into a state of hopeless confusion. The Khyberees taking advantage of this disorder, ham-strung many of the camels, and thus secured the loads as a booty. The escort having with some difficulty, and the loss of a few men, succeeded in repulsing their daring assailants, returned to Peshawur, minus about five hundred camels and a quantity of baggage, which fell into the hands of their enemies. The commissariat, previously much straitened for carriage, now declared that they had not the means of carrying the supplies requisite for the march.

A detachment, consisting of all the infantry of the column, (altogether six companies, including one of the European Regiment,) were now ordered to march to Ali Musjid, and occupy that fort, until relieved by a party from the army in Afghanistan. Colonel Wheler's brigade of Native Infantry was ordered to move from Jellalabad into the Khyber pass; and thus the defile being entered by the two forces from opposite sides, would be swept throughout, and a fair probability presented itself of chastising and bringing to terms the daring banditti.

Colonel Wheler's advanced guard was attacked by a body of Khyberees at the crest of the steep descent into the valley of Lumdeekhana, but the marauders, seeing the columns advance in force, soon gave way, and retired to the interior of the hills. Subsequently, some of the Khyberee chiefs came down to hold a conference with Colonel Wheeler, their followers burning fire with the Sepoys in token of amity; and much regret was expressed for the injuries which had been sustained at the hands of those chiefs who *had not* been bribed. On arrival at Ali Musjid, Colonel Wheeler found the detachments from Peshawur in the fort, to which they had penetrated with a few supplies, after another skirmish with the Khyberees, in which, however, the marauders were roughly handled.

The chiefs had promised that on the payment annually of one lakh of rupees, the passage of the Khyber should be kept open to the British; and it was supposed that matters were finally arranged with the Khyberees, but upon terms which did not sound agreeably in a soldier's ear, though, politically speaking, they might be deemed expedient.

Matters having been brought to the conditions named above, by those who were empowered to treat, the infantry brigade, accompanied by the detachments from our column, which had been relieved, now proceeded towards Peshawur. The troops had advanced but a short distance from

Ali Musjid, when a swarm of Khyberees once more rushed from the heights, and, pouncing upon the baggage, succeeded in carrying off a number of camels, principally laden with the officers' baggage, which they drove up one of the numerous ravines communicating with the main passage of the defile. The rear-guard, which had probably been overlooked by the plunderers, immediately gave chase; and having been reinforced by parties from the detachments which occupied the heights flanking the ravine, who had witnessed the theft, came up with the Khyberees, and having committed considerable havoc amongst the traitorous rascals, succeeded in recovering some of the camels and their burdens. The troops then proceeded on their route to Peshawur, which was reached without any further molestation.

Such was the state in which we abandoned Afghanistan. Having marched victoriously throughout the country, and thrust a monarch upon his reluctant subjects, the ill-fated Shah Soojah, with ill-disguised apprehension, beheld himself placed on the throne of a hostile country supported only by too much weakened British regiments, a few sepoys, and a small body of half-disciplined Hindoostan levies. The Bombay division, on their return march, had found an enemy in nearly every

mud-fort, and met with a spirited resistance from
Mehrab Khan at Khelat; whilst the Khyber Pass,
the direct gate of communication with our far-
distant provinces, closed behind the Bengal
column as soon as it had crossed the threshold.
The savage and marauding Khyberees, reckless
of all faith and treaties, continued to commit
numerous deeds of rapine and violence, thus
amply proving, had any proof been required of
such a self-evident fact, that these treacherous
bandits were only to be restrained from their
hereditary profession of plunder whilst their
mountain-fastnesses were being actually swept by
an overwhelming military force; yet, in opposition
to these stubborn arguments, political agents were
yet to be found who advocated, and endeavoured
to adopt, conciliatory measures.

In Dost Mahomed's time, the Khyberees had
little or no temptation offered them to infringe
their agreement; but the sight of the baggage
which accompanied our column was too much for
their resolution.

The garrison of Ali Musjid, having been left
in unenviable quarters, and our fellow-soldiers
in Afghanistan to enjoy themselves as they might
in their isolated situation, we prepared to resume
our march, and traverse the remaining four hun-

dred miles, which lay between us and our advanced posts on the frontier of Ferozepore.

The infantry detachments, which had lately been engaged in the Khyber Pass, had not rejoined, but followed shortly afterwards, whilst the first column proceeded onwards through the valley of Peshawur.

On the morning of the 20th of November, we proceeded on our march, and encamped a few miles distant from the city. At this place, in the broad daylight, a party of plunderers from some adjacent hills came down and carried off many camels, which were grazing at little more than a mile from the lines. The rear-guard of the Lancers, immediately on the alarm being given, turned out in pursuit, and from a small knoll in camp, we had a favourable view of the chase.

The robbers, amounting to about forty, having got a good start, were pushing for the hills, about five miles distant from camp, and driving the camels before them at a round pace, pricking the bewildered animals forward with the points of their lances and cimeters. The dragoons gained steadily on them; but a few men of the irregular cavalry hung closely on their flanks and rear, and although they were too few to obstruct effectually the retreat of the banditti, yet they compelled them to abandon several stray and restive camels. As they neared the hills, the eagerness of the pursuers redoubled, and the camels dropped fast to the rear, bearing on their flanks severe marks from the weapons of their merciless captors. At length, the robbers, with the residue of their booty, were close to the foot of the hills, the dragoons were still half a mile behind, and the irregular horsemen, who were less than two hundred yards off, drew up, and gave a parting fire from their matchlocks, but without effect. With a shout of exultation, the mountaineers wheeled about to return the fire, when two gallant fellows from the irregular horse, dashing round their flank, threatened an impediment to their line of retreat. The chances seemed, for a moment, to be against the bandits, for none of them appeared willing to encounter their daring opponents, and whilst wavering at the foot of the heights, the dragoons had come within a few hundred yards. Choosing the least of two evils, the marauders, driving the remainder of their booty before them, rushed, *en masse*, upon the unfortunate irregulars, who were unhorsed, but unwounded, ascended the hills, and dispersed in many directions amongst the gullies and ravines which intersected the face of the mountains.

Barely a dozen camels were altogether secured by the marauders out of nearly a hundred which had been seized. During the pursuit, many villagers from the plains turned out to offer assistance; for these mountaineers are unfriendly neighbours to the agriculturists, and scruple not, when urged by necessity, to take whatever may be useful to them from the unwarlike and helpless dwellers in the plains.

From hence, crossing an extensive plain, we encamped near the banks of the Caubul river on some greensward, and under a grove of trees.

This was a most luxurious day's residence, and the prospect was more English than anything we had hitherto seen in the East, or perhaps I should have rather said, Irish, for the mud huts of the country bordering Peshawur bear a close resemblance to Irish cabins, although the unclean animal, that prominent feature at the threshold of most dwellings in the Emerald Isle, is here considered an unwelcome guest.

A traveller desirous of conciliating the natives of this country must needs be choice in the selection of animal food; for in this district—from Peshawur to the Jhelum river—dwell the Mussulman population of the country, whose abhorrence is a pig; across that boundary the imperious Sikhs look with pious horror on beefeaters, for one of their deities is a bull. The pea-fowl and pigeon are also held in much veneration by the Sikhs, notwithstanding the ungodly voice of the bird of Juno, and the destructive habits of the sacred pigeons. The allurements of immortality, however, compensate for the loss of temporal possessions, and the depredations of the sacred fowl are viewed with indifference, and by the more devout, with satisfaction.

On leaving the Caubul river, we passed again over tracts of desolate plains and barren hills, until we reached once more the banks of the Indus, on the 26th of November, at the fortress of Attok.

About a mile above Attok, the Caubul river forms a junction with the Indus, and the united streams rush with great rapidity in a deep and narrow channel under the walls of that ancient and gloomy fortress. A temporary bridge of boats had been thrown across the Indus, opposite to the gates of Attok, which enabled us to cross the river without much delay, at the end of the morning's march. At this season, the breadth of the river did not exceed one hundred and fifty yards, and the cavalry crossed the bridge without dismounting.

From the approach on the Caubul side, Attok presented rather a formidable appearance, with its extensive and massive parapets frowning over the dark floods beneath; but at the junction of the two rivers, about one mile higher up, a passage might easily be effected with a pontoon train, where the guns of the fort would be nearly inoffensive. When once landed on the left bank, the fortress would not present a very formidable obstacle, for the hills immediately above the town afford an excellent position, whereon batteries might be placed which would command both the town and fort at a range of something less than six hundred yards.

The Sikhs were very jealous of admitting any of the officers within the fortress; but as the best view of the place was obtained from the hills above mentioned, this reluctance on their part did not cause us any disappointment, and the much-vaunted stronghold of Attok was generally admitted to be a fortress of no importance, with regard to its present strength and site. Had a strong detached work been placed on the upper range of hills, it might have rendered the position more tenable, although the whole rampart of the place being exposed to view from the opposite bank, must soon be made to succumb to the stroke of a heavy battery. Such a catastrophe, however, could never have been expected from the Afghan quarter, as their battering trains are not of the most effective description.

A merchant from India had arrived here with wines and other luxuries, which, in addition to some we had procured at Peshawur from another enterprising merchant, *en route* for Caubul, introduced us once more to those dainties with which previous experience had taught many of us cheerfully to dispense.

Proceeding on our march from hence, I looked in vain for the fertile land of which I had heard and read; the appearance of the country near our line of march was but little superior to Afghanistan.

The tract between Peshawur and the Jhelum river is almost entirely occupied by the Mussulman population of the Sikh territories, from whom Runjeet Singh levied his Mussulman regiments, which are generally supposed to have been the most efficient of his army.

The natives of this part of the country are not supposed to bear any particular good will to their neighbouring masters, and were kept in strict subjection by Runjeet. To quell their martial spirit, and diminish the chances of a revolt, they were restricted from wearing arms, whilst in the Punjaub almost every Sikh may be seen following the plough with the singular encumbrance of sword and shield—at least, in that part of the country bordering on the Mussulman districts.

Should a rupture ensue between the British and the Sikhs, there is little doubt that if the war be carried into the heart of the Punjaub, this ill-will on the part of the Mussulmans may be turned to our advantage; for it is generally supposed that the immunity offered to their religion and habits under the British rule, would induce them to prefer it to their present state of subjection.

Six marches from Attok brought us to the celebrated Tope of Manikyala, in which a vast quantity of coins were recently discovered.

This place is supposed to be the Bucephalia of Alexander's time, by Mr. Ventura. Its modern name of Manikyala may appear to warrant such a supposition; but as the Bucephalia was placed on the right bank of the Jhelum, to command the passage of the river, Sir Alexander Burnes has objected to the site. This I deem an inconclusive objection, for the reasons already assigned in page 214.

The monument at Manikyala is a massive spheroidal building of stone and brick. The perimeter of its base exceeds three hundred yards; its altitude was computed at something more than fifty. On reaching the summit, by the aid of some rude and time-worn steps, we found an aperture, resembling a dry well, which descended apparently to the foundation of the building. This well was searched, some years ago, by General Ventura, and at the bottom was found a box, containing many valuable coins, and also a phial, filled with some liquid.

Whilst peering into this cavity, a tall Sikh, who had arrived on the same spot, stood watching me with that inquisitive stare which, at first blush, excites the sufferer to anger, but which experience had now taught me meant nothing more than simple curiosity.

" Has the sahib discovered any curiosities below ?" demanded the intruder, as I rose from my occupation.

" No; but perhaps you can enlighten me on the subject of this huge pile, and as to your native traditions of the architect and his intentions," I replied, in mongrel Hindustani, which this native was intelligent enough to comprehend.

" I was here some years ago," he answered, " when General Ventura searched this well and discovered many ancient pieces of gold, and silver, and copper. The mound has stood here many centuries, before the Sikhs possessed this country, and is generally supposed by the country-people to have been erected by Shah Sikunder (Alexander the Great) as a monument over some one of his generals, who, probably, fell in battle near this spot. Our architects declare that the monument was of a foreign origin."

Such was the pith of the information given by my heathen companion, as we descended together from the building by the rude staircase, constructed, perhaps, by the hands of Macedonian engineers and masons, and trodden by the foot of the invincible Alexander, whose mighty deeds and conquests, although they have transmitted the deathless name of the conqueror to posterity, have failed in assigning a definite spot to his achievements here, or in marking the limit of his advances into Hindostan—if, indeed, he ever did penetrate as far as those realms—if, alas! that after a whole life devoted to the pursuit of the phantom, Ambition, (which was, probably, nearer the grasp of the Macedonian than that of any subsequent devotee,) the attainment of his favourite project, the conquest of the East, should at this day remain a matter of uncertainty. Such is fame, and so much worth, that gnawing and unaccountable desire to live in the memories of posterity, which animates alike the poet, the statesman, the soldier, and the philosopher, to a life of labour, anxiety, hardships, or study, that his name may survive when the body has partaken of the common lot of mortality, and lies insensible alike to the worms which are gnawing the flesh, and its fellow worms above who are probably toiling to destroy that reputation which was the fond and nurturing object of its earthly career.

The keenest satire on ambition which I have read, lies in the observation of Horace—

> " Expende Annibalem, quot libras in duce summo
> invenies ?"

But let the cynic sneer his fill at the desire of distinction during life, and the cravings for a name with posterity; such is the indefinable condition of the animal, man, that I firmly believe no mortal ever existed who could despise the prospect of their attainment. Such are the uncertainties which attend human attainments and foresight, that a heathen fanatic has, at one fell swoop, destroyed the labours and monuments of ages of literature,* and left the very existence of many sages of antiquity to be called in question: and the stupendous pyramids, on which the suns and storms of unknown ages have beaten, still rear their aged crests into the serene sky, whilst the object and even the names of their projectors remain a matter of doubt and dispute.

Whilst indulging these sombre reflections, at the foot of the Tope of Manikyala, my reverie was interrupted by the approach of a Sikh, who displayed some coins for sale, which the first glance assured me were spurious. Reader, be not alarmed; after this dissertation on the novel topic of the vanity of human forethought, I will not indulge you with a treatise on the still more uncommon theme of dishonesty. I will merely add, that I returned the Sikh his coins, telling him that they were worth a trifle under their actual weight in copper, and then adjourned to a breakfast which the impatience of two brother officers had made cold and scanty. The village of Manikyala has been so completely denuded of antiquities, by the diligence of European tra-

* The library of Alexandria was destroyed by the Arab, Amrou, a few years after Mahomet. Abulphuragicus Dynast., p. 115. This is questioned by Gibbon, (!) vol. iii. p. 478, quarto edition.

vellers, that not a coin of any value was found there by any of our party.

As we proceeded, a barren country still surrounded us, intersected, in the most singular manner, by deep ravines, which appeared to have been caused by heavy floods from the mountains. So frequent, deep, and precipitous are these rents in the soil, that even were the natives ever so industriously disposed, the culture of such a surface would be attended with great disadvantage, both on account of the infertility of the soil, and the difficulty of tillage and communication.

Having descended into the dry course of a river, we pursued its sandy track nearly to the banks of the Jhelum river, which is better known under its classical name of Hydaspes.

About thirty large flat bottomed boats had been collected at the small town of Jhelum, on the right bank, for the transport of troop baggage, as also for the soldiers themselves, if it were deemed requisite; but the river was supposed to be fordable about half a mile above the ferry of Jhelum, and the ford, which was about four hundred yards in width and very tortuous, was designated by several bamboos placed upright in the stream to mark the course to be pursued in crossing.

An officer was sent to report on the practicability of the ford, (the officials from the quartermaster-general's department having already crossed in boats,) who crossed and recrossed on horseback, and reported the greatest depth to be about four feet, and that his horse had kept his legs firmly during the passage. The Lancers then received orders from the brigadier to cross on horseback, and entered the river by sections of threes. The advanced party, keeping close to the canes which marked the ford, reached the opposite bank in safety; but the mass of the column, when within about a hundred yards of the left shore, lost the indications of the ford, which had probably been destroyed by the advance, and, on diverging from the track, the greater part were immediately out of their depth. The line of demarcation being thus trampled over and lost sight of, nearly the whole regiment, yielding imperceptibly with the current, got below the proper ford, and, seeing no further marks to direct them, pushed indiscriminately for the nearest landing-place. First one poor fellow, on a weak horse, was swept away by the current; and, unable to extricate himself, encumbered as he was with heavy accoutrements, soon lost his seat, and being struck by the horse in his efforts to stem the current, sunk, and was seen no more. Soon afterwards several more, mostly mounted on animals which were too feeble* to swim with the heavy weights on their backs, were seen struggling in vain to make headway, until, exhausted with their endeavours, they parted company; and the Dragoons, unless strong swimmers, were soon overcome, whilst their horses, when freed from their weights, swam wildly down the river. Amongst the victims was Captain Hilton, commanding the fourth squadron, who, being a heavy man, unable to swim, and mounted on a weak old Arab charger, sunk almost without a struggle. The confusion which prevailed may be easily imagined, and it appears wonderful that so many managed to reach the shore. The boats employed in the transport of baggage, being all heavily laden, could move but slowly towards the scene of disaster, which was more than half a mile distant from most of them, and it was only by working up near the bank and thence pushing into the stream that they could have reached the spot; but they were unable to do so until all was nearly over, and few, if any, escaped by their

* The greater part of our horses had not regained much strength after the sorrowful work and starvation they had encountered during the recent campaign.

assistance. Those men who had succeeded in reaching the shore now vociferated confused advice to their comrades in the water, each loudly recommending some designated place of safety, whilst those struggling with the current were unable to catch a single word of advice or command from their numerous advisers, on account of the rushing and stunning din of the stream, and the clatter of surrounding voices. When the greater part of the regiment had reached the shore, a body of the strongest swimmers stripped themselves of their encumbrances, and hurried to the assistance of their comrades, many of whom were nearly exhausted by their efforts to keep above water, or benumbed with the cold, which, at eight o'clock on a December morning, is severe, even in this latitude.

Numbers of camels, which had attempted a ford rather higher up the river, with heavy loads on their backs, had been carried off their legs, and these, floating down the river amongst the soldiers, were the means of saving many a poor fellow's life, by affording him something to cling to until he could be rescued from that precarious situation by the vigorous exertions of his fellow-soldiers.

Soon after the regiment had crossed, it was

mustered on the banks, and Captain Hilton and ten men found missing. The bodies of Captain Hilton and six men were found in the course of the morning, and interred close to the river, but the bodies of the remaining sufferers were not recovered during our halt at the fatal Jhelum.

Had we been compelled to cross this river in the face of an enemy, the ford could not have been more boldly attempted than on this occasion.* Because a single horseman had crossed in safety it was deemed advisable that a whole regiment should do the same, neglecting the probability of the alluvial deposits in the bed of the river been trampled to the consistency of a quicksand by such constant and heavy pressure. As a sufficient number of boats had been collected to transport the whole regiment, with their horses, across the river within the space of a few hours, it is difficult to assign a reason for plunging into so deep and uncertain a ford, with a rapid current and an unstable footing.

Major Hough, the diffuse historian of Indian

---

* In the month of April, upwards of two hundred years ago, Jehangire's army forded this river with a force of Rajaputs opposing them. Many were drowned, and most of the remainder fell into the hands of their enemies. (Dow's India, vol. iii., p. 81.)

warfare, has informed us "that the commander-in-chief and staff regarded the distressing scene with feelings of the deepest commiseration;" which must have been very consolatory to the drowning men, and doubtless the survivors are duly grateful to his excellency for such a flattering display of humanity.

CHAPTER XI.

HAVING thus floundered through the Jhelum, we
had passed the boundary of the Mussulmaun, and
entered the Sikh division — i. e., the Punjaub.
The Punjaub is bounded on the north-west by
the Jhelum river, and not by the Attok, as
usually marked in the charts. The five rivers,
from which it derives its name,* are the Sutlej,
the Beeas, the Ravee, the Chenab, and the Jhelum.

The country did not exhibit any sign of improvement until we neared the Chenab, being
mostly overgrown with long dry grass, not un-

* Punjaub means, literally, five rivers.

like that which covers some of the prairies of America. But it cannot be a matter of surprise, that the inhabitants should pay more attention to war than agriculture ; had it been otherwise, they would have sown only for the hardy and warlike inhabitants of the neighbouring mountains. A nation must be great in war ere it can hope to flourish in commerce and agriculture, or the nest will surely be robbed ere the progeny be full-grown and able to defend themselves—or rather, capable of learning that useful art.

The cold of a winter's morning in India, though much less severe, of course, than that of more northern latitudes, is still very smartly felt on the line of march, for it is necessary to march in the morning, to enable the cattle to go out and graze after their work is over.

Mounted on a charger, who is forbidden to deviate from a walk during a morning's march of twelve or fifteen miles, with the feet in a pair of heavy iron stirrups, and a keen blast driving the cold dust through the half-frozen patient, is the daily lot of the soldier on a winter's campaign in the East. With anxiety he looks forward through the morning's gloom for the first peep of dawn ; but no sooner has the merciless sun attained a few degrees of elevation, than he exhibits a fiery aspect which soon renders the shadow of a tree or a fold of canvas by far the most interesting object in the view. Whilst the European, clad in his tight and cumbersome costume and accoutrements, toils wearily onward under the fiery noon-day heat on a long march, the Asiatic warrior, divesting himself of a portion of his flowing dress, twirls the light material round his head, and under its grateful shadow encounters lightly and cheerfully the task which lies before him. The graceful Oriental turban serves the invaluable purposes of guarding the head from sun and cold, of defying the edge of the sabre, and arresting the progress of a bullet; the European head-dress answers no useful purpose : cannot the ingenuity of England's hatters suggest some plausible scheme for defending the susceptible sculls of their countrymen serving in India? Verily, if they cannot accomplish that object, they deserve, and may they continue to enjoy, the imputation of insanity.*

Five marches from the Jhelum brought us to the banks of the Chenab; of the depth, rapidity, and means of transit over which, about as varied and accurate reports had been received as were transmitted on our arrival at the Jhelum.

* " Mad as a hatter," is a favourite term of comparison.

On reaching the Chenab river, we encamped within a few yards of the bank; and as the fortunate discovery was soon made that an abundance of boats were in readiness, the greater part of the baggage was taken across in them during the day, and next morning the regiment embarked.

The camels, when unloaded, as also the horses, with a native groom (or " syce," as they are termed) on each, were enabled to cross at a ford, about two miles down the river, which was more than four feet in depth. These natives, being light weights and unencumbered with trappings— for the saddles and all their weighty concomitants travelled in boats—took the horses across the ford without any accident or difficulty. Nor was there any risk in the experiment, for most Orientals swim soon after they have learned to walk.

The country now assumed a much more cheerful and civilized appearance : crops rose luxuriantly on each side of our line of march; and the well-inhabited towns and villages told of an abundant, though not a very wealthy* people, for the mud houses were little, if at all, better than those of Hindostan.

* The chiefs take care to provide for this. Colonel Ford, a British officer in Runjeet's service, had three villages given him for pay, out of which he was allowed to make the most. This was the usual practice ; but the people are now growing stronger.

Ofttimes, the massive and circular tomb of some Mussulman, now falling fast to decay, (or in many instances, the ruthless hand of time, having evidently been assisted by the unsparing jealousy of the bigoted Sikhs,) glared upon us from out its gloomy and sepulchral shade of banyans. Since the date which some of the buildings tried to commemorate, the haughty Mussulman conqueror had yielded to the more arrogant Sikh idolator, who must soon give place, in the inevitable cycle of events, to a milder and more tolerant power.

These white and spectral monuments failed not in their object of attracting observation, whilst the fretted and ostentatious carving apprised us of the earthly resting-place of bones probably belonging to some proud grandee, who had played his little part on the stage of life, and whose deeds done in the flesh, though failing to rescue his name from oblivion, had succeeded in earning a monument to become an asylum of refuge for rats, owls, and jackdaws. This is as it should be, when—

> " Some proud son of man returns to earth,
> Unknown to glory, but upheld by birth."

Since leaving Attok, we had been accompanied by an escort of Sikhs, under Sirdar Lana Singh.

who, it was expected, would have met the commander-in-chief on the frontier with an invitation to visit Maharajah Kurruk Singh (the reigning monarch of the country) at Lahore. Lana Singh being vested with no such authority, our original route, which lay through Lahore, was altered, and the force proceeded by a road which left the capital about fifteen miles to the East.

With a nation so punctilious in points of etiquette as the Sikhs had hitherto been, the fact of allowing the British forces to approach within so short a distance of their capital, without sending a deputation to wait on the commander-in-chief with an invitation to their court, betokened a slight which told plainly the ambiguous relations existing between the Lahore government and the British. The most probable cause of this omission was, that both the authority and intellect of Kurruk Singh being feeble, and the court itself in a turbulent and unsettled state, the ministers were unwilling that the British should be eye-witnesses of their present state of anarchy.

Dhian Singh, the prime minister, had always testified an aversion to the British, even in the days of Runjeet, according to Mr. Prinsep's account, and there is little doubt that this marked neglect was owing to his suggestion. Had they valued, or wished to court our friendship, as the old Lion of Lahore had ever done,* they would not have been thus tardy with their invitation, or at least, they would have made some apologies for the maharajah's inability, from ill-health or some other invention, to be honoured with an interview.

On the present occasion, we had arrived within fifteen miles of Lahore without any communication from the durbar, and at a small town named Budee, when late in the afternoon a party deputed by the Sikh government entered our camp, bringing the commander-in-chief the tardy courtesy of a request to visit the capital. Instructions having been received from the governor-general of India, conveying a desire that Sir John Keane should, if possible, visit the maharajah, the scanty ceremony was overlooked, and the commander-in-chief, escorted by the 16th Lancers, a troop of horse artillery, and a few native infantry, diverged from the route, and proceeded next morning towards Lahore, whilst the second column, under General Thackwell, continued their route by the more direct road to Ferozepore.

Having made two marches over an uninteresting country, speckled with patches of long dry

* The disposition of Eastern states, like the character of froward children, may be tested by these trifling humours in their behaviour.

grass and underwood, we arrived on the banks of the Ravee, and encamped close to the walls of Jehangire's tomb.

The city of Lahore lay about four miles distant, stretched along some gently rising ground on the opposite shore of the Ravee, but we could barely discern its locality owing to the haziness of the atmosphere. It was Christmas day, and decidedly the least merry one I can remember having passed. The gloom rivalled that of London at this period of the year; the clouds occasionally indulged us with a smart shower of rain, which, under canvas, is the most uncomfortable weather imaginable, especially when accompanied, as this was, by a piercing easterly wind, which swelled in the folds of our tents, and defied all efforts to exclude the noisy intruder. In the afternoon, the weather having cleared up a little, I visited the Emperor Jehangire's tomb, in company with a brother officer. We entered the extensive building by a gateway leading into a large square court, the four sides of which were pierced by a succession of small casements, each divided into two cells, which would have made very comfortable quarters for a Dragoon and his horse.

Calculating on the probability of their being ere long devoted to some such purpose, we found that the square would have well accommodated a cavalry regiment at its full strength. Crossing this yard, we passed under a lofty, arched gateway, and entered the gardens in which stood the tomb of the Emperor: a massive square building, of about thirty feet in relief, from the four angles of which rose the usual flanking parties, lofty and handsomely carved minarets. In the interior, we found nothing costly or worthy of note. On a platform of white marble steps, in the centre, stood the sarcophagus, made of the same material, whose sides had been chipped and defaced by the Sikhs, to exhibit their magnanimous contempt for the deceased Mussulman potentate. On ascending the exterior of the monument, we found the flat roof paved with stones of various colours, which had a singular effect, the whole constituting a pattern of great dimensions. As none of the stones were of any value, and all pretty tightly fastened with cement, the natural indolence of the Sikhs had saved this part of the structure from injury. On ascending one of the minarets, whence an excellent view of Lahore may be obtained on a clear day, we observed, at the further side of the garden, a small conical tomb, built to the memory of the far-famed, beautiful Nourmahal, wife of the Emperor Jehangire. Her pathetic and marvellous

history has formed a theme for many relaters of
tales throughout the east; but for the enlightenment
of the few whose ears they may not have reached,
I will give a brief sketch of the adventures
assigned to her lot.

Nourmahal was the daughter of a ruined Tartar
chief, and was born in the desert between Tartary
and Hindostan when her parents were emigrating
to the latter country. Overcome by weakness
and fatigue on the journey, they found themselves
unable to carry on the infant, and Nourmahal was
left to perish where she was born. The mother,
after deserting her child, was so overpowered with
grief as to be unable to proceed, whereupon Aiass,
the father, returned in search of the infant, which
he found encircled by a large black snake. The
reptile fled at his approach, and Aiass, finding to
his surprise that the infant was uninjured, brought
it to the mother. A caravan, shortly after, opportunely arrived, and relieved them from their dis-
tresses; and, without difficulty, the whole party
reached Lahore, which was then the seat of
government of the Moguls conjointly with Agra.
Aiass having found a relative amongst the Omrahs
of the Emperor Akbar, obtained, through that
influence, a place in the household of the monarch,
and rose in time to wealth and distinction. His

daughter, who was called Mher el Nissa, (the sun of women,) possessed unequalled attractions of beauty, and was also remarkable for wit and accomplishments—a rare combination for an Eastern beauty.

Selim, the son of Akbar, being present at an entertainment given by Aiass, was much attracted by Mher el Nissa's graceful figure and voice; and the accomplished beauty, having *accidentally* dropt her veil, discovered to the happy prince such charms as had never before shone upon the eyes of man. Poor Selim, who was as much in love (as the Asiatics fictitiously term a passion of which they are ignorant) as a prince could be, applied to the Emperor Akbar to obtain for him the beautiful toy he had beheld. It was discovered that Mher el Nissa was betrothed to the Omrah Sher Afken, a Turcoman noble, who might be a dangerous enemy, and Akbar refused to employ harsh measures to dissolve the contract. The disappointed prince was therefore compelled to defer his passion and projects till a more convenient season, and Mher el Nissa became the wife of Sher Afken. After the lapse of a few years, when Selim had ascended the throne under the name of Jehangire, Sher Afken left the court and retired to Burdwan. He was recalled from thence by Jehangire to the court then held at Delhi, and the monarch testified so much regard for the Turcoman chief, that he very naturally concluded that all was sincere and disinterested on the part of Jehangire.

At a royal tiger-hunt which took place, the noble beast was marked down in the jungle, and Jehangire, knowing Sher Afken's character for strength, personal courage, and love of adventure, demanded that volunteers, to meet the tiger single-handed with a sword, should present themselves; four came forward, Sher Afken amongst them, and, whilst the others were contending for the precarious honour, the Turcoman Omrah offered to face the tiger without a weapon. Jehangire, with inward joy and outward reluctance, assented. Sher Afken advanced to the lair, and man and beast rushed into each other's clutches. The tiger made some use of his claws, and mangled his opponent; but he had to do with a hero of romance and not a mere mortal, consequently the complaisant beast submitted, and allowed himself to be strangled. The fame of Sher Afken rose with this exploit; he recovered from his wounds, and became much honoured by the people and petted by the monarch, who had many similar adventures in store for him. An elephant was sent to crush

Sher Afken in his palanquin. The hero arose, and, with one blow of a *short* sword, cut the elephant's trunk asunder at the root, and killed him on the spot. Forty hired assassins tried to murder him during the night; he slew twenty, and generously allowed the remainder to escape. Sher Afken seems at last to have discovered that Mher el Nissa was the object of Jehangire's persecutions, and as it is considered a foul stain on a man's honour in the East to part with any of his wives, the troublesome husband retired with the sun of women, to his private residence at Burdwan. The chief of that Bengal province immediately received instructions to remove the modern Uriah to a better world, and, approaching under the pretext of a tour of inspection, but with a large retinue, the king's official visited Sher Afken, who met him unattended. The royal party soon proceeded to business; but Sher Afken having pulled down an elephant and castle, slain the emperor's agent, and killed a nobleman at every blow, was at last surrounded by archers and matchlock men, who galled him from a distance. He did not condescend to fall before his horse was killed, and six bullets, and arrows innumerable, had perforated his body; then, discovering he was mortal, the gallant and devout Omrah turned towards Mecca, threw sand on his head, and began to die. The soldiers dared not approach until he was in his last agonies. The party then hastened in search of Mher el Nissa, fearing that in the first outburst of regret for her irreparable loss she might wish to accompany her deceased husband to Heaven; but happily she was less overcome than they expected, and appeared resigned to her fate, declaring it was entirely out of regard to her husband, that he might be immortalized by his wife becoming afterwards Empress of India, that she submitted to become Jehangire's sultana.

On her arrival at Delhi, to her surprise and mortification, she found that some caprice of Jehangire not only assigned her the most paltry rooms in the seraglio, but left her to poverty and neglect. The emperor did not even visit the woman for whom he had stained his name with indelible crimes.

Mher el Nissa, with laudable indifference, amused herself with embroideries, (in which art she excelled,) and her talents in this humble occupation soon brought her name into notice. After four years spent in this manner, it appears that curiosity weighed more with Jehangire than boyish love, for he stole to the apartments of the beautiful embroideress to witness her toil. The result is evident, for none could look on this dangerous beauty unmoved. The next day, the Emperor Jehangire celebrated his nuptials with Mher el Nissa, under the title of Nourmahal, (the Light of the Harem,) which was afterwards changed to the more dignified and affectionate title of Sultana Noor Jehan. The sultana continued to enjoy her husband's confidence, and forms one of the few instances in Eastern history of a queen being acknowledged more powerful than her lord.

By her influence, her father became prime vizier, and was renowned for his virtue and abilities in office; but, unhappily, her influence over Jehangire was afterwards exerted to produce less creditable and less fortunate results.* She survived her husband for upwards of seventeen years, which serves to account for the paltry tomb erected to her memory.

On the morning of the 26th of December, we crossed the Ravee in boats; but the horses, as well as the camels and other beasts of burden, were able to ford the river without being unloaded, the Ravee being much narrower than its two predecessors which we had crossed.

* For further information, I refer the reader to Dow's "History of India."

Shortly before mid-day, we arrived within a mile of the city, and encamped in a ploughed field, the advantages of which position were by no means enhanced by the fall of rain on the previous day. The weather now promised to be fine, luckily for us, and the ground was soon dried, and as soon levelled by the constant intercourse with Lahore. Immediately on our arrival, intimation was received that we must consider ourselves all as guests of the Sikh government, who would not admit of our purchasing any of the daily supplies requisite in camp; and it was requested, that a return might be furnished of the strength of the escort, that provision might be made for ourselves and cattle. This daily distribution of provender was continued during the remainder of our sojourn in the Punjaub, up to the day we recrossed the Sutlej. Heaps of grain, straw, grass, eggs, flour, &c., were piled every morning in front of the commissariat-officer's tents, and beside them, droves of sheep and poultry stood, awaiting their fate with bleating and cackling sorrow.

This singular practice of feeding the troops of their allies was no novelty on the part of the Sikhs; the same custom prevailed during former visits of British embassies to the court of Lahore, in the lifetime of Runjeet Singh.

A memorandum was issued shortly after our arrival, recommending the officers to abstain from visiting Lahore, until Sikh guides had been obtained, as a sort of safety escort; it was, at the same time, notified that sundry long-bearded savages would shortly be waiting at the commissary-general's quarters, for the benefit of any officers desirous of keeping such company.

This recommendation was neglected by many, in their impatience to visit the celebrated metropolis; and though, generally, the Sikhs behaved with unusual civility towards us, there were not wanting some examples of the contrary.

The approach to Lahore from our camp was certainly the most favourable point of view which could be procured. An extensive plain, covered with turf, and enlivened by occasional clumps of trees, is stretched along the exterior of the city-walls in this quarter; and the view of temples, barracks, minarets, arsenals, and battlemented-walls, jumbled in thick and confused order behind the ramparts, announce to the visitor that he is about to enter a city which has maintained no inconsiderable part on the stage of Eastern history. As I rode towards the city-gate, in company with another officer, a party of some twenty Sikh horsemen were issuing from the portal. On perceiving us, they levelled their long spears, and advanced towards us at full gallop. I could not refrain from forthwith drawing my sword, to meet this unprovoked act of aggression; but my companion, whom experience had made acquainted with Sikh peculiarities, requested me to ride unconcernedly forward, and pay no attention to them. When this adventurous body of cavaliers arrived within two or three spears' length of us, they checked their horses back upon their haunches, tossed up the points of their lances, and dispersed over the plain, indulging in loud shouts of exultation at such an unwonted display of horsemanship and courage. I could not help thinking, that had I been alone, and provided with the usual furniture in my holsters, the noisy occupants of two saddles might have paid dearly for this uncourteous display of activity to a stranger. However, it is better for both that such was not the case.

Having crossed the bridge over the moat which defends the ramparts, we entered Lahore through a series of narrow, dirty bazaars and lanes, thronged, as usual, with inhabitants, yet so narrow, that three horsemen could not ride abreast, except where some monument or temple had been erected, in front of which the thoroughfares had been widened and improved. It was with some difficulty that we made our way amongst the crowds of people, who gazed at us more intently than if we had been wild beasts in cages. The only recompence for this troublesome curiosity was a good view of the fair-complexioned, dark eyed damsels, who occupied many windows and balconies on the first story. As these exalted beauties had the consideration to appear unveiled, we had ample opportunities of admiring their charms.

Having caused so much sensation, we almost began to imagine that hitherto a wrong estimate had been formed of our importance, and that we really were not what we thought; but, unhappily, our rising notions of greatness were sadly checked by the discovery that we were merely regarded as curiosities, but did not possess even sufficient influence to gain admittance to the arsenal.

The Sikhs were very jealous of allowing any of the officers of the escort to visit their military establishments. In one of the temples converted into a barrack, we were anxious to ascend a tower, which must have commanded a good view of Lahore, but the sentry was inexorable. We applied to the officer in command of the barrack, but he pretended that the doors were locked, and the keys mislaid. This apprehension of gratifying our curiosity was no matter of surprise, although the precaution was useless, as we were not likely to benefit by the sight of their military institution; and as Lahore, in its present state, is incapable of defence as a fortress, the view enjoyed by two officers on the summit of one of its towers would not have tended much to endanger the safety of the city and its inhabitants.

This complaint of the Sikhs' jealousy was made by nearly all the officers who visited the city, though many had gone with influential natives as an escort.

Sir John Keane having been for some time suffering from illness, which prevented him from quitting his tent, a deputation of officers from head-quarters waited upon Kurruk Singh, in his palace, to tender excuses for his excellency's inability to see the maharajah.

There was little display of magnificence or of munificence at this Durbar compared to those which had taken place in the days of Runjeet; and it was evident now that the paw of the old

Lion of Lahore had relaxed its grasp of authority, there remained little respect for the present puppet-show of royalty.

Each officer attending the Durbar was presented with a dress of honour of an average value of about two and sixpence sterling, and the damaged Cashmere shawls presented as nuzzurs, would have been mean offerings to send home to our respectable grandmothers. I have particularized those reverend ladies, because their taste in the selection of that elegant and becoming head-dress, the Cashmere turban, might enable them to roll out of sight many of the defects of Kurruk Singh's presents, which would have been fatally glaring when spread on the shoulders.

Notwithstanding the enormous importation of shawls from Cashmere into the Punjaub, the difficulty of procuring a really rich and handsome shawl is greater than is commonly supposed. The most valuable are generally purchased by the wealthy natives, who have the best opportunities of procuring them; secondly, a good judge is required for the selection; and, thirdly, rupees to spare to the amount of from five hundred to twelve hundred, for the purchase of each.

The day after the Durbar above named, Kurruk

Singh, attended by his court, visited the commander-in-chief at his tent. As some busy gossips among the Sikhs had circulated a report that Sir John Keane's illness was merely a pretext for withholding his company, and thus evincing disrespect for the maharajah, Kurruk Singh and several of his party were invited to enter the sleeping apartment, which they did, and doubtless were convinced that the report of his excellency's aristocratic disorder was not without foundation. Presents having been made, and the usual forms and conversation having been conducted by means of the interpreter, (Captain Powell,) the variegated mass of silks, birds'-feathers, and jewellery, arose and departed. As this shuffling crowd of Kurruk and his courtiers moved, bowing their heads, through a lane of some two dozen brawny, square-built Englishmen, drawn up as a guard of honour at the doorway, I could not forbear a smile at the ludicrous contrast in manner and bearing, as well as the unusual spectacle of the royal family of the Punjaubees, bowing and cringing to the brave and sturdy descendants of some hard-working British artizans.

Let these arrogant Asiatics crow as they will

during our absence, it is very clear that they cannot refrain from evincing their mighty respect for British prowess when brought into contact with it.

I always have, and still do entertain, the highest prepossession for good blood and breeding, both in man and beast; nor was I staggered in my opinion by this day's exhibition. It only tended to exalt the estimate of my countrymen, for I should prefer the plainest drop of English blood to the turbid streams flowing through the veins of the proudest descendant of the Prophet, precisely as I should select a sound English hack in preference to the weedy and stumbling offspring of the best Hindustanee parents.

Whilst accompanying the maharajah's party across the plain, between our camp and Lahore, I observed some Sikhs engaged in their favourite diversion of hawking, which being a novelty to me, I joined the party, and rode with them some distance in pursuit. A noble falcon had been slipped, and was in full chase of a kite, much larger and probably stronger than himself. The falcon had no easy game to play; he practised several dextrous manœuvres, and stooped with great rapidity; but the quarry was equally wary, and cleverly avoided the enemy's attack, though his inferioity in speed prevented him from contending successfully when soaring for the higher place. At length, night put an end to the contest, and the bird having been called in, we rode homewards; but the kite, after his exertions, must have been ill qualified to procure an evening's meal.

The Sikh sportsmen behaved with civility, and took some pains in conveying instructions to me in falconry; but I derived little benefit from their attentions, not being able to understand one-tenth of what they said. Their knowledge of Hindustani appeared to be more limited than my own, and one prevalent error was using the nose as much as the mouth in the course of their conversation. I am not sure that I am justified in calling this an error; for the Americans, who contend that they speak English better than we can, adopt the same mode of pronunciation. Their literature and social refinement must add weight to the assertion. Washington Irving, by far the first of American authors, complains of the ignorance and prejudice of English writers on America: let me give him an example, taken from a book written by an American of a learned profession. His opinion is not confined to one country, and caused me a good hearty laugh. The author having become intimately acquainted with the

misery and ignorance of European nations, pro-
ceeds to pronounce sentence at the end of his
book—the only good part:

" My soul has been sickened at the sight of
oppression, ignorance, abjectness, and vice, which
I have seen everywhere the result of arbitrary
rule.* I contrast with these the general intelligence, the independent spirit, the comparative
virtue of my countrymen, and I am proud of the
name of an American. But it does not become
us to boast.† True greatness *never* plays the
part of the braggadocio. If the people under the
despotic governments of Europe are less intelligent and happy than we, it is their misfortune,
and not their fault, and they are more deserving
our pity than our scorn!!" ‡

I think we should be at a loss to find a parallel
for this amongst the most ignorant and prejudiced
of our writers on America.

On the morning of the 28th of December, we
quitted Lahore, having discharged the required
duty of visiting Runjeet's unworthy successor,

---

* N.B.—Arbitrary rule, in his vocabulary, is explained to
mean, simply, any monarchy or empire.

† The author has made this discovery too late, and the next
sentence seals his fate.

‡ " Two Years and a Half in the American Navy," vol. ii.
p. 244.

and witnessing the estimation in which he was held. The party of Sher Singh (the next in succession to the throne) was supposed, at that time, to be strong; and the death of Kurruk Singh, which occurred shortly afterwards, is generally attributed to a plot to bring the favourite to supreme authority. But the death of Runjeet rang the death-knell of the nation he had brought to such rapid importance.

The reign of Kurruk's successor commenced with the massacre or removal of most of the European officers in the Sikh service, by the soldiery; the natural consequence of which must be the deterioration of that discipline which Runjeet wisely devoted the greater part of his life in endeavouring to establish. Could he have deputed his own abilities to his successor, the Punjaub might have risen into one of the most important nations of the East; but the army is becoming daily more disorganized and under less control. Their arrears of pay remain unsettled, which is a dangerous experiment; and the officers, although possessing little authority with the troops under their command, are among the disaffected. They are becoming troublesome neighbours on the north-western frontier, especially as their country is so situated as to interfere with our direct communication with the far-distant and isolated position in Afghanistan. Under these circumstances, they must necessarily be made either permanent friends or obedient subjects; they will never become the former, and it will take a good many years to reduce them to the latter alternative; yet, if we continue to hold Afghanistan, it must be done.

At a distance of about six miles from Lahore, we passed the camp of the main body of the Sikh army, consisting of about fifty thousand men and one hundred and sixty pieces of cannon. Having pitched our camp about four miles distant from this overwhelming host, we were invited by Sher Singh to attend a review of the army, which he directed to be held that afternoon.

On reaching their camp, it was already so late, that we had only time to ride along their line, (which extended to an enormous distance,) before sunset. Some of our officers, who had been with the previous mission to Lahore, remarked regiments apparently of recent equipment. On approaching the end of the line, torrents of abuse were lavished on the British nation by the chivalrous Alkalees, who brandished their weapons, shook their quoits, and behaved with incredible valour, if not rashness, in exhibiting to four or five strangers and visitors what a dangerous and formidable class the Alkalees were, and how much they detested the Feringhees, even without knowing them.

These besotted fanatics, we were told, had done the old Lion some service, when, excited by opium and exceeding pot-valour, they dashed headlong into the ranks of their adversaries, who, being less intoxicated than the Alkalees, or less capable of directing the effects of their intoxication, gave way in confusion before these accomplished drunkards. More worthy symbols of superstition could hardly be found amongst the Fakeers and idiots* of the Hindoos.

The new regiments of cavalry, which appeared to have been equipped or raised since our last rencontre at Ferozepore, were a brigade of lancers, (a laughable caricature of the British regiment, which they were intended to resemble,) two corps of cuirassiers, and some mail-clad irregulars; the latter uncommonly fine, rough-and-ready looking fellows—light troops which, well-handled, would cause much inconvenience at outpost or guerilla-service, unless their appearance belied them. I was told by an officer of an ingenious

* An idiot is revered by the Hindoo, as a Heaven-afflicted sufferer.

device which he saw practised by the Sikh infantry. When wheeling into a parade-line, a string had been laid on the ground, which was invisible to a looker-on at a short distance, and when the word of command was given, each regiment wheeled up to this mark, and thus formed a pretty correct line without any trouble in dressing or posting markers. The evening closed in so soon at this season, that we had little time afforded us to observe their progress in manœuvring, as the extensive line toiled through the manœuvre of changing front, whilst the artillery enveloped the whole scene in dust and smoke. The Sikh artillery is, however, beyond a doubt, the most effective branch of their service, working with great rapidity, and firing with almost as much precision and regularity as the British, who have been their model.

During the progress of this review, three or four officers, having left their horses in charge of some Sikh soldiers, mounted the elephants which had been sent by the Sikh sirdars as calculated to give a better view of the field than could be obtained on horseback. The review being over, these officers, returning to the spot where their horses had been left, found, to their dismay, that chargers, horse-trappings, and Sikhs had vanished. Search amongst such a host of men and beasts, in the dusk of evening, presented very small chance of success; so, endeavouring to reconcile their minds to the severity of fate, they returned to camp. A complaint of the loss was immediately forwarded by the British political agent to the Sikh authorities, who promised that the horses should be recovered or their owners indemnified. During our halt at Ferozepore, a few days afterwards, the horses were restored to their owners, mainly owing, it is supposed, to the enormous value attached by one of the officers to an animal of decidedly unprepossessing appearance, whose unaccountable value and good qualities were possibly known only to his master. The Sikh thieves had been palpably ignorant of the value of their prize; for this extraordinary charger, (though always belonging to the lean kind,) had now been suffered to dwindle away until he became a close resemblance of an engraving which I remember having seen, a few years ago, in the London engravers' windows, entitled, " The Nightmare." The facetious quadruped is represented with its head tied to a knocker, and grinning in the face of the alarmed house-owner, who appears at the

door dressed in his night costume, with a rush-
light in his hand and a blunderbuss under his
arm.

Several more petty thefts were committed on
our camp whilst in the vicinity of the Sikh army;
and in some instances the dexterity of the thieves
was not inferior to that of the many renowned
practitioners throughout Hindostan.

Four days march from the Sikh camp brought
us once more to the banks of the Sutlej, which
we crossed in boats, re-entering the provinces at
the point from which the army had started on this
long and wearisome tour. Ferozepore, which we
had left a mean native town, was now embellished
with extensive, white-washed bazaars; and a neat
little fort in the centre of the town was occupying
the attention of our engineers. The ground,
which had been covered by the canvas-abodes of
a portion of the army at the close of the year
1838, was now, in January, 1840, the site of a
large cantonment, which had risen, as if by magic,
within the space of fourteen months, and was
then tenanted by three regiments of native infantry and some artillery.*

From hence, we shortly afterwards dispersed

* A fort on modern principles was soon after built in cantonments, and quarters provided for a British regiment.

in different directions, to occupy our allotted quarters. We marched through Khytul and Kurnal, to occupy our former quarters at Merut, which we had no sooner reached, than the excitement of the campaign being over, the sufferings and privations which all had undergone began to tell severely upon their health, and many a gallant fellow was committed to his last resting-place in the sombre burial-ground of Merut.

END OF VOL. I.

T. C. Savill, Printer, 4, Chandos-street, Covent garden.

CPSIA information can be obtained
at www.ICGtesting.com
Printed in the USA
LVOW11s1130060717

540276LV00001B/45/P